La Vacanza

La Vacanza

Bernard Moscardini

Spiderwize

La Vacanza

Spiderwize
Mews Cottage
The Causeway, Kennoway
Kingdom of Fife
KY8 5JU
Scotland UK

www.spiderwize.com

ISBN: 978-1-907294-27-3

In memory of Mother who sacrificed so much to feed and protect her children.

~

In this autobiographical account, all the events relating to the author and his family and relatives did in fact happen as described.

Chapter 1

I was nine years old. Little did I realise when Mother and I set off on that unforgettable spring day at the beginning of May 1940 for our annual summer holiday in Italy, that our departure was to mark not only the start of the longest 'holiday' of my life, but also a momentous period in the lives of my entire family.

I was born in Bedlington, a small mining town in southeast Northumberland. In our family there were five of us in total: Mother, Father, my brother John who was six years older than me, and my younger brother Aldo who was born in the autumn of 1940.

My parents both originated from a small Italian hilltop village called Sommocolonia, in the province of Lucca. Life was very difficult in Italy at the turn of the Twentieth Century and especially in the mountainous regions of northern Tuscany.

Both my parents had emigrated to England at the beginning of the Twentieth Century in search of a better way of life. My mother emigrated with her family when she was a small child. My father came over to England in his twenties in order to work for his older brother Federigo.

My uncle Federigo had originally intended to emigrate to America. When he presented himself at the port of Genova to board the ship bound for America, the authorities informed him that he could not be accepted because he was too young; he therefore decided to try his luck in England. And so it was, that he went to work for a Mr Pieroni, an Italian from the Barga region, as a *garzone* (a sort of apprentice dogsbody).

Mr Pieroni had started a business consisting of an ice cream parlour, confectionery and tobacco products in Stanley, County Durham. He soon found that business was thriving and was thus able to open a second shop. With two shops to run he needed plenty of help and this was how he came to employ Federigo and another chap from the Barga region called Mr Vincenti.

Mr Pieroni had for some years secretly dreamt of an early retirement to his native town of Barga in the province of Lucca. With two successful shops he soon began to amass a considerable sum of money in his bank.

At that time, the rate of income tax in the UK was very low, sterling was the premier currency in the world, and there were no foreign exchange restrictions.

In the early 1920's Mr Pieroni reckoned that he had made sufficient money to last him for the remainder of his life and he decided to sell up and return to his native land to enjoy the fruits of his hard work. He therefore sold his businesses to my uncle Federigo and Mr Peter Vincenti, who set up in partnership.

Mr Pieroni's early retirement was no doubt encouraged by Federigo Moscardini and Peter Vincenti who were both eager to be given the opportunity to run their own business. When Mr Pieroni retired he bought a large villa in Barga with a view to spending the rest of his lifetime in blissful peace. He soon found, however, that without the help of a regular income, his accumulated capital was slowly but irrevocably diminishing.

Within the short period of six or seven years he realised that he would have to get back into business if he did not want to spend his later years in penury. He then returned to the UK where he set up once more in business, this time in Ashington, Northumberland. It is most probable that he was also encouraged to take this course of action by the fact that he was finding the humdrum life of retirement rather boring. Now he was not only back in business but he was also the owner of a large house in his native town of Barga.

The business arrangement between my uncle Federigo Moscardini and Peter Vincenti did not last very long, for, after a period of about two or three years, they dissolved their partnership and each of them branched out on their own. Now that Federigo had his own business he was able to send for his brother (my father) to work for him as a *garzone*. He later also sent for their cousin Vittorio Moscardini.

My mother's parents had established a very thriving business in Blaydon, County Durham, selling confectionery, tobacco products and ice cream. When my parents were first married they helped run the family business in Blaydon for a number of years, and it was here that my older brother John was born.

It had always been my parents' ambition to eventually branch out into business on their own. Therefore, in the late 1920s, Mother and Father, with the financial help of my maternal grandparents, purchased an established business from a Mr Rinaldi, who himself was also from Sommocolonia. This business was in Bedlington Station, a district of Bedlington. The correct name was really Sleekburn but it was known as Bedlington Station because of its railway station, which served the Bedlington area.

The business that my parents took over was a Temperance Bar, which was rather ironic, bearing in mind that my father was a copious drinker and he frequently returned home quite inebriated after a night out in one of the local public houses. The shop consisted of an ice cream parlour with confectionery and tobacco products and, later, it also incorporated a small café.

Before World War II my father made his own ice cream by hand. Like most other Italian immigrants at that time he could not afford to purchase any expensive automatic ice cream making equipment. Making large quantities of ice cream by hand was a very laborious task. Father had to constantly make up a refrigerant consisting of a mixture of ice and salt. I clearly remember the large blocks of ice, which were regularly delivered for this purpose.

Bedlingtonshire was right in the heart of the southeast Northumberland coalfield. In its heyday there were more than a dozen collieries in the shire and coalmining was the main occupation of the area.

I have very fond memories of those pre-war years. My parents ran a reasonably prosperous business, and, although it wasn't a goldmine, it ensured a very comfortable standard of living for our family.

Despite the fact that I was born during the period of the great depression, I wanted for nothing. There was a lot of poverty in working class areas at that time. The mining community was particularly badly afflicted by the depression and its wretched effects were evident everywhere. Many of the miners' children went around poorly dressed, sometimes in ragged clothes and with shoes full of holes. I, on the other hand, was always very well dressed and neatly turned out.

Apart from material wealth, we were always able to afford medical care which had to be privately financed in the days prior to the establishment of the National Health Service. As a result, our health was not neglected due to lack of money.

This was just as well for I had been quite a sickly child and had often needed recourse to medical attention. The most likely explanation for my almost constant ill health was probably due to the fact that I was not generally allowed to play outside, in the dirt, like other children. In this way I had never built up a natural immunity to many diseases.

Since my parents ran a retail confectionery business, it meant that I always had access to lots of goodies. Confectionery was normally sold loose in those days and I loved to wander behind the shop counter. There, I would frequently help myself to sweets and chocolates. A particular favourite of mine were the 'marzipan diamonds' in the Milk Tray selection manufactured by Cadbury. The marzipan centre was green and to me it was the ultimate delight.

And yet human beings never seem to be satisfied. Despite being surrounded by a plentiful supply of free sweets and chocolates, I would often sneak into the railway station across the road to buy a penny bar of Nestlé milk chocolate from the vending machine in the station concourse. At that time Nestlé chocolate was not available in sweetshops in our region, and was only sold through vending machines.

The very thin Nestlé penny bars of milk chocolate seemed to taste even more delicious than the usual chocolates and, besides, I loved the thrill of putting a penny in the slot and pulling out a bar of chocolate. I would quickly eat this chocolate before returning home because I was quite sure my parents would not have approved of these clandestine visits of mine to the railway station.

I was not encouraged to mix with other children although I was allowed to bring home into the flat above the shop a boy called 'Spud'. His real name was Kenneth Thompson but, for some strange reason, he was known as 'Spud' as were his father and his brother.

Kenneth's father was a butcher by trade. He had originally set up in business on his own but he had unfortunately fallen on hard times as a result of the depression, which had hit the local mining community very hard.

Mr Thompson had been far too generous in helping out the families of his unemployed customers with free meat on the promise of paying him back whenever they could. There were some, of course, who never had any intention of paying him back but the majority of honest folk who made up his clientele simply had no means of repaying their debts.

Mr Thompson soon went bankrupt. He and his wife had six children and it was inevitable that they had great difficulty in feeding and clothing their family.

Across the road from our family business there lived another Italian family called Bacci who ran a fish and chip shop. Mr & Mrs Bacci had one child, a daughter called Nita, who was about the same age as my brother John. Nita loved to organise games and races in the back lane behind their fish and chip shop. It was here that I got to know Kenneth Thompson whose family lived in our back street 'sports stadium'.

Every few weeks Nita would organise a kind of mini sports day. This would consist of various games and races up and down the back lane. The competitors would comprise the Thompson children, my brother John and myself. Nita would purchase lots of little prizes and we would all participate most enthusiastically in all the events and have great fun. I loved those sporting occasions, which were always special and full of excitement and joy.

Kenneth's family lived in a small terraced house, two up and two down. They had no bathroom or hot water and their toilet was situated outside, across the back lane. The Thompsons were not the cleanest of people and their home was really a bit of a hovel. I remember that their house always had a peculiar malodorous smell.

Kenneth's parents always seemed to be rowing, frequently using some of the foulest language I have ever heard. I did not often go to their house to seek Kenneth, but whenever I did I would not linger any longer than necessary.

With such poor conditions in the Thompson household, Kenneth enjoyed coming to our house where he liked the clean surroundings of our flat. He also knew that it was a place where he would be well fed. Kenneth became a very close and loyal friend of mine over the years.

Sadly, Kenneth died of alcohol abuse at the age of thirty-four. As a child he had contracted rheumatic fever which had left him with a weak heart. Kenneth was found lying in a field unconscious and covered in frost on New Year's Day 1964 after consuming a rather large quantity of alcohol to celebrate Hogmanay the previous evening. Despite all efforts to revive him, he died without regaining consciousness.

For some strange reason I was encouraged to join the school choir in my primary school. Whatever musical talents I may have had then, as a vocalist, they certainly did not persist in my later years. In fact during my late teens I was categorically told by one of my teachers that I was completely tone deaf.

On one occasion in 1938 our school choir was chosen to enter a singing contest in Morpeth, Northumberland. It was a very grand occasion with about six or seven other choirs participating in this music festival. We were taken to Morpeth by coach and were accompanied by the head teacher and several other adults. I felt so important for we were all dressed in our finery.

That afternoon when we got back to the school after the concert, there was Kenneth, standing outside the school gates, waiting for my return. He had been waiting for a good couple of hours and he looked quite forlorn. He soon cheered up when he saw the coach arrive.

On Sundays, which was the busiest day of the week for the business, Kenneth and I would be left to our own devices in the flat above the shop. I used to love to play tricks on people in the street. Motor vehicles were few and far between in those days and a maximum of about five or six vehicles would pass along the street in the course of a typical Sunday.

I had this big motor horn, the type with a rubber bulb, which you had to squeeze. I believe that it was a spare horn from one of the two horse-drawn ice cream carts that Father ran. When pressed, the horn would emit a very loud raucous sound.

I would lie in wait till a group of people was casually meandering across the street. Then I would lean out of the upstairs window of the flat and squeeze the horn as hard as I could. I never failed to be amused at the sight of those people hurriedly jumping out of the way of a phantom vehicle.

One Sunday, whilst playing with Kenneth in the flat, I began to mess about with the pepper pot. The lid suddenly came off and the ground pepper spilled all over the plush red 'Sunday' table cover. I quickly cleared up as best as possible and replaced whatever pepper I could, back into the pot.

Then I did a very foolish thing. I rubbed my eyes and got pepper in them. The pain was really excruciating and the resulting noisy commotion quickly brought Mother up to see what was happening. She got really cross and, although she did not smack me, I received a very severe scolding. It had been a most salutary lesson for me. After that I made sure that I never fooled about with pepper again.

My most vivid recollections of those days were of the Christmas parties at the local primary school. How I used to really love those parties with the presents and the large illuminated tree, the games and the Christmas carols.

My parents never believed in, or perhaps never had the time, to organise parties for my birthdays. In fact, during the whole of my childhood, I never once had a birthday party. I suppose that this was one of the main reasons for my anticipation and subsequent enjoyment of the magical atmosphere of the school Christmas parties.

On the advice of his brother Federigo, Father set up a billiard saloon, which he ran along with the main shop. He had very boldly bought a plot of land and, with the help of a considerable bank loan, had constructed a row of three small shop units with a large hall at the back of these buildings. The three shop premises were rented out and, in the hall, he opened a billiard saloon, with six tables.

His timing could not have been better. Billiard saloons were quite popular in those days. They did not require much expertise to look after and running expenses were very minimal.

The unemployed miners had lots of free time on their hands and they could frequent the billiard hall without having to spend much money. A game of billiards or snooker or pool cost only a penny and this was just the perfect form of entertainment for men who could afford little else.

In the billiard hall there was also a kiosk which sold soft drinks (by the glass), ice cream, sweets and tobacco products. Business boomed right from the start and although my father's bank loan was quite considerable for those days, he was able to repay the bank within the short space of six or seven years.

By law, the billiard hall could not open on Sundays, which was ideal because Sunday was the busiest day of the week for the Temperance Bar.

The outbreak of war in 1939 affected everyone's life. Among other things blackout curtains were compulsory and everyone had to adhere to the blackout regulations.

The billiard hall had a large expanse of glass roof to let in plenty of daylight. With the possibility of air raids, these large sheets of glass could pose a very serious problem. I remember that they had to be painted black and had to be fitted with black sliding blinds.

There was also a fear that the Germans might bomb Britain with gas, and each person was issued with a gas mask. Even children had their own individual gas mask. Gas masks had to be carried by everyone at all times in case of a sudden surprise attack by the enemy. At my primary school, concrete air raid shelters were built and we held regular rehearsals in these shelters wearing our gas masks.

One day during a routine air raid practice, a boy in my class suddenly had a panic attack. He had just put on his gas mask when he irrationally began to fear that he was going to choke. He tried to pull off the rubber mask but, the more he pulled, the more he gasped for breath. It was only after the intervention of our teacher that he finally managed to calm down.

This had quite an unnerving effect on all the children in my class. I myself had never really liked wearing a gas mask and, after this incident, it terrified me every time we had to proceed to the air raid shelter wearing gas masks.

Ironically, there was one slightly pleasing thing that came out of the outbreak of war in 1939 for me. My older brother John had been learning to play the pianoforte for about two years. The music teacher would come to our house about twice a week, and John hated these lessons.

As Christmas approached, it was going to be my turn to have piano lessons and I was dreading the thought. As it turned out, my fears were unfounded because the piano teacher suddenly stopped coming to our house and that was the end of the music lessons.

On making inquiries we found out that the piano teacher was now in the Armed Forces. He had either enlisted or he had been conscripted. What joy! I did not have to worry about piano lessons any more.

Nowadays, with hindsight, I very much regret the fact that I did not have the opportunity to learn to play a musical instrument in my younger years.

Mother, Mrs Bacci, Nita Bacci, Bernard & John. Circa 1937.

Mother & Father. Wedding photo. Circa 1924.

Mother's family. Uncle Dino, Grandmother Adele, Grandfather Giovanni Marchetti. Mother seated. Circa 1913.

*'Tea-break' in Stanley Co. Durham. Circa 1920. Giuseppe Moscardini
(Dad), Federigo and Vittorio Moscardini.*

John Moscardini.

Aldo Moscardini.

Aunt Dora's wedding in 1939. Bernard Moscardini is the pageboy.

Chapter 2

R ight from an early age, it had been the custom that every year, my brother John and I, would go on holiday to Sommocolonia with Mother to meet all our relatives. We would usually go for the duration of the summer holidays, and occasionally at other times of the year.

I remember one particular year going over immediately after Christmas. This was very lucky for me because I had two lots of presents that year: the normal presents for Christmas in England and another set of presents on the day of the Epiphany. It was the custom in Italy then that children got their presents on the sixth of January in commemoration of the Magi bearing gifts for baby Jesus.

A good fairy called *La Befana* would bring the presents. In fact I believe that even to this day it is still the tradition in some catholic countries for children to receive their presents on the sixth of January.

There were many songs that Italian children sang about *La Befana*. These varied from region to region. The version that I learnt as a child was the following:

> *La Befana vien di notte,con le scarpe tutte rotte.*
> *Col cappello alla romana. Viva, Viva la Befana.*
> *La Befana vien di notte, con le calze tutte rotte.*
> *Con le toppe alla sottana. Viva, Viva la Befana*
> *La Befana vien di notte. Dentro il sacco ha il carbone.*
> *Ma anche le caramelle. Viva, Viva la Befana.*
> *La Befana vien di notte. Scende giù dal tuo camino.*
> *E ti porta un regalino. Viva, Viva la Befana.*
> *Ecco arriva la Befana.*
> *La Befana vien di notte con le scarpe tutte rotte.*
> *Sta guardando dal camino, se già dorme ogni bambino,*

se la calza è ben appesa, se la luce è ancora accesa.
'Zitti, zitti, presto sotto le lenzuola'. Ecco arriva la Befana.
'Li chiudete o no quegli occhi?'
Se non più che buoni, niente giochi né balocchi.
Solo cenere e carbone.

La Befana arrives at night, her shoes full of holes and
wearing a Roman style hat. Three cheers for La Befana.
La Befana arrives at night, her socks full of holes and
lots of patches on her skirt.
Three cheers for La Befana. La Befana comes at night.
In her sack she carries coal.
But she also has some sweets. Three cheers for La Befana.
La Befana comes at night, climbing down your chimney.
And she brings you a little present. Three cheers for La Befana.
Look La Befana is arriving.
La Befana comes at night, with her shoes full of holes.
She is watching from the chimney, to see that every child is
sleeping
Is your sock hung up correctly, is the light still on?
'Hush be quiet under the sheets'. La Befana is arriving.
'Are you going to shut your eyes or not?'
For if you're not really good, there'll be no games or toys,
just coal and cinders.

So here we were setting off again for our customary holiday in Italy: my maternal grandmother Adele, my mother, who was five months pregnant, and myself.

John had decided not to come with us this time. He was almost fifteen and had reached that age when boys are not keen on going on holiday with mum. Besides he reckoned that Father needed his help, for both the billiard hall and the temperance bar were starting to get very busy. Now that Great Britain was at war the country needed lots of coal and consequently the miners were back in full employment.

Everyone had assumed that Father had sent us off to Italy so that Mother could conclude her pregnancy and give birth in a region well clear of the harshness and rigours of war. Whatever might happen, surely Sommocolonia would be a safe and quiet retreat up in the mountains of the *Garfagnana* region? What an irony, for we were eventually to end up in the thick of the fighting right in the front line.

It was also well known that Father was very patriotic and he very dearly yearned to have an Italian son. As my brother John and I were both born in England, it was most probable that this was a further reason why Mother had been sent to Italy: to give birth to an Italian child.

The journey to Italy was a bit of a nightmare to say the least. The ferry crossing was quite terrifying, for the English Channel had been mined. Everyone was issued with a life jacket as they boarded the ferry at Dover. We had to wear these life jackets for the whole duration of the crossing until we arrived and docked in Calais.

The sea was very choppy that day and people were being sick all around us. This coupled with the fear that the ferry might possibly hit a mine made me very apprehensive. Fortunately all went well. We arrived safely in Calais where we boarded the train for Paris.

In Paris we had to change stations. On arrival at the *Gare du Nord* we caught a taxi to take us to the *Gare de Lyon*. This latter station was a bustling hive of activity; there were French troops in full battledress milling about everywhere. There was a distinct air of impending doom and all the talk was of the war.

I was not really old enough to appreciate the seriousness of the situation. For I could not realise that Hitler's troops were in fact sweeping through France at that very moment and, that a few days later Paris would fall into the hands of the advancing German army. Nevertheless, I could sense that something terrible was about to happen.

In contrast the rail journey to Pisa was quite uneventful. When we arrived in Italy, there was the same foreboding air of impending disaster as in Paris. Everyone was talking about the situation in Europe and rumours were rife about Italy entering the war as an ally of

Germany. Mother became quite disturbed by all these rumours. About ten days after our arrival I remember going down to Barga with her to the travel agency to try and book our passage back home to England.

Barga was, and still is, the small administrative town (*Comune*) of the area. In a recent census, a total of just over 10000 inhabitants had been registered as living within the *Comune*.

During the Middle ages Barga had had a very chequered history. It was a typical fortified hilltop town constantly warring with neighbouring towns and cities. Its defensive walls had three gateways. Of these, only one, *Porta Reale* has survived into modern times fairly intact.

As Barga occupied a strategic position for the trading of goods between the regions of Modena, Coreglia, Garfagnana and the Versilia coast it became an important market town in those days.

It was not far from Sommocolonia as the crow flies. Yet it took us the best part of an hour to travel the five or so kilometres on foot. As soon as Mother expressed her request to Mr Tognarelli, the travel agent, he shook his head and replied: (*Mi dispiace Signora, ma è troppo tardi!*) "I am sorry Madam but you are just too late! All the borders through France have just recently been closed. Had you come last week we could have booked you back home but now it's impossible." And that was how we came to 'enjoy' a protracted holiday, which was to last for over five and a half years.

Nevertheless Mother was determined to find a way to get us back home to England at the earliest possible moment. Rail travel was the chief means of transport in those days. Scheduled air services had not yet been really developed. The only other possible alternative was by sea. Mother started considering this option but there were no regular shipping services between Italy and the UK. It might be a long time before we would be able to board a ship to return home.

And so we just had to wait and see what might develop and we didn't have to wait long. Some days later an announcement was made over the news media that *Il Duce* (Mussolini) was going to make an important speech on the *Giornale Radio* (radio news) at one pm on the tenth of June.

None of the villagers could afford the luxury of a wireless set and so there were only two radios in the village. The first belonged to the priest. It was not the done thing in those days to go along to the *canonica* (rectory) and ask the priest if we could listen to the news.

The second radio set was in the *Dopolavoro*, a working men's club where men (but not women) could go and relax in the evening and have a drink or two after work. Mother therefore decided to go down to Barga to hear what *Il Duce* had to pronounce.

In the *Piazza del Comune*, in front of the *Café Capretz*, a loudspeaker had been set up to relay the momentous news to the people. The *Piazza del Comune* was literally jam-packed. I will never forget listening to *Il Duce* declaring war on England during that broadcast. The deep staccato tones of his voice almost penetrated my inner soul.

Most of the people began to cheer for *Il Duce* had a great charismatic effect on the Italian population. I myself did not fully comprehend the import of this speech for my knowledge of Italian was limited to only a few words relating to the family and the home. I was also too young to understand the consequences of this declaration of war.

Despite this I knew that something awful had happened and that we would somehow be adversely affected by it. We could now say goodbye to being able to get back home to England in the foreseeable future.

About ten to fifteen days later we got quite a surprise when my mother's sister, my aunt Dora, suddenly arrived from England without any warning. She had been advised by her husband, Joe (Beppe) and her stepfather, Mr Saporiti, to try to get a passage on the ship which was going to repatriate the Italian Ambassador to England, along with other diplomatic staff.

Dora was not very keen on this course of action. The seas were all mined and she certainly did not want to undertake such a hazardous sea journey. Furthermore she had no idea what she might encounter in Italy.

Her husband Beppe and her stepfather Mr Saporiti had eventually managed to persuade her that, whatever might happen, she would undoubtedly be safer in the quiet little backwater of Sommocolonia if ever there was to be a bloody conflict. She was extremely lucky to be able to get a passage on that ship.

Dora's arrival was accompanied by a moving and emotional family reunion. She was very welcome indeed and she was treated like a long lost relative. We greatly appreciated the company of another member of the immediate family. As it turned out she not only boosted our morale but was also able to help out Mother in looking after Grandmother Adele. Also Mother was by now six months into her pregnancy and would soon be needing help herself. Furthermore, Dora brought with her all the latest news from England.

Chapter 3

Dora was undoubtedly my favourite aunt. She was rather short in stature, somewhat chubby with a round face, which always sported a welcoming smile: the very epitome of a cuddly aunt. She was the youngest of the three Marchetti children: my uncle Dino was the eldest, then came my mother Dina, and Dora was the baby of the family.

My aunt Dora was always very kind to me. This may have been because she did not have any children of her own. It was indeed with great surprise and incredulity that I learnt from her in later years that she had in fact been quite a naughty rebellious child.

My maternal grandfather, Giovanni Marchetti, was not the sort of person to tolerate such behaviour and, despite my grandmother's protests, he decided to send Dora to Italy to be educated. In those days the men always dictated family affairs; women, more often than not, had to concur in silent acquiescence.

Dora was therefore placed in a convent school for girls in Lucca. She thoroughly hated it because it was a very strict boarding school. In fact during the three years in the convent she was only allowed the occasional weekend away. She had to spend these weekends with a family called Simi, in Lucca.

Although Signora Simi was Dora's aunt, the family were complete strangers to her. She also had to spend the school holidays with the Simi family in Lucca. This meant that she never saw her parents for three years.

Dora was quite a lot younger than Mother. In those days the Italian immigrants were a very close knit community and as such very rarely even attempted to integrate into the local population. As a consequence Italian women were invariably expected to marry Italian men.

These were not arranged marriages as such, but they all knew what was expected of them. My uncle Dino had naturally married an Italian girl. I gather that Mother had in her late teens fallen in love with an Englishman. Because of the long established tradition of marrying within the strict boundaries of the Italian community she had had to suppress her strong feelings in this matter. And that was how she came to marry Father.

Aunt Dora was therefore sent over to Barga on holiday in 1938 to look for a prospective bridegroom. Several suitors presented themselves and among these a chap, called Beppe (Joe) Lunatici, particularly impressed Dora. Joe was a fairly tall man with a moustache and quite handsome to boot: altogether an ideal Latin fiancé.

My uncle Joe Lunatici was one of ten children. His parents had had a very hard struggle bringing up such a large family, especially as the employment situation was very grave in the Barga area. In fact the only employment Joe had been able to obtain was as a part-time *barrocciaio* (carter).

In financial terms Dora was considered a 'very good catch' in those days. When Mr Joe Lunatici realised that Dora was seriously interested in him, he did not hesitate. He saw this as his opportunity to get away from all the poverty of the region and seek a new and more prosperous life abroad.

After a reasonably short courtship, they were married in the spring of 1939. It was one of the biggest Italian weddings they had ever seen in the northeast of England. The reception was held in the Old Assembly Rooms in Newcastle-upon-Tyne. There were well over 300 guests, a considerable number for a working class marriage at that time.

My aunt had six bridesmaids and two pages, one girl and one boy. I was the page boy all dressed in white satin. It was indeed a memorable day for me and I remember feeling ever so important. I thought I was "the bee's knees" as I strutted around in that white satin outfit.

Many of the Italian men would come over to me and pat me on the head saying *bel ragazzo,* lovely boy. They were all in business either running their own shop or working as *garzoni* awaiting the chance to set up on their own.

One of the men made a very public display of slipping half a crown (2 shillings and sixpence) into my hand. If there is one thing Italian men dread, it is *fare una brutta figura* (being shown up or outdone by others). And so, many of the other men also placed half a crown into my hand.

I ended up that day with well over ten pounds, a considerable sum in 1939 for a little boy. My mother kept relieving me of all the coins saying that she would look after them for me because she was worried that I might lose them. I don't think I ever saw that money again.

My maternal grandfather, Giovanni Marchetti, was a very heavy drinker and, not unnaturally, he died at an early age through overindulgence in alcohol. He had been warned several times by his family doctor that if he did not stop drinking, he would soon die.

The year he died he had gone over to Italy with his brother for the express purpose of seeking expert medical advice. The Italians living in England all believed, rightly or wrongly, that Italian medical expertise was best. There was certainly a greater degree of mystique surrounding medical specialists in Italy at that time when compared with England.

The two men journeyed to Florence to seek the opinion of a *professore*. After examining my grandfather, the specialist informed him that he could do nothing at all for him. His liver was irrevocably damaged and it was only a matter of time. He died only a few weeks after returning to England. I never in fact knew him because he died many years before I was born.

Grandmother Adele later married another Italian called Mr Saporiti. As a child, I remember Mr Saporiti as quite an imposing person who commanded great respect. He resembled very much the film star Edward G. Robinson in so many ways: in physical stature, looks and deportment.

Mussolini's declaration of war on England meant that all the Italian nationals living in the UK became enemy aliens. When the news was heard in Bedlington a large band of local people began to gather outside the business premises in Bedlington Station and started to break the windows. They kept shouting for my father to come outside, intimating that they were going to 'string him up'.

Several people did not particularly like my father. It undoubtedly stemmed partly from xenophobia but it was also probably due to jealousy of his success in business. Added to this, Father was a staunch patriot and very proud of his Italian nationality.

Although he was not a paid up member of the Fascist party he had always been a very fervent admirer of Mussolini. I remember that a large photograph of *Il Duce* took pride of place on the wall above the fireplace in the flat over the shop. This may possibly have been one of the main reasons for his unpopularity.

Whether this unruly mob would have really killed my father is a matter of speculation for the police soon arrived to restore order. They immediately arrested my father and took him away to intern him as an enemy alien. He was eventually taken, along with many other Italian nationals, to an Internment Camp on the Isle of Man, where he remained for the best part of the war.

Father was indeed very lucky to be interned in the Isle of Man. The British authorities had decided to deport some of the alien internees to Canada. The liner Arandora Star that had been commandeered for war service, was one of the vessels used for this purpose. On its first voyage this ship was not displaying any visible signs that it was carrying enemy aliens. And so, on the second of July 1940, a torpedo from a German submarine hit the Arandora Star and she sank off the Irish coast.

On board, there were over 700 Italian nationals and nearly 500 German nationals. Of these 486 Italians and 175 Germans lost their lives. Among those who perished was Mr Saporiti's brother.

When the police arrived to arrest Father, my brother John, who was only fifteen, was absolutely terrified. The police advised him that, although he was a British subject, it would be wiser if he did not remain all on his own in the flat above the shop. So John telephoned his cousin, Virginia Moscardini, in Stanley, Co. Durham. Virginia said that she would come and pick him up the following day. She advised him to meanwhile find somewhere to sleep that night.

John then went to stay with the Bacci family across the road. Mr Bacci had been arrested along with Father, but Mrs Bacci and her daughter Nita had temporarily been allowed to remain in their house.

Women enemy aliens were not normally interned, but the regulations stated that they had to reside in an area a minimum number of miles distant from the coast. This apparently was to prevent them from communicating with any enemy ships or submarines. Consequently Mrs Bacci and her daughter had to move further inland within a few days.

The next morning Virginia arrived in Bedlington Station by taxi to pick up John and take him back with her to the Stanley home. At Stanley my uncle Federigo had also been interned despite the fact that his two eldest sons had volunteered for war service and were serving in the British Army. My aunt Fernanda, who was an Italian national, had been forced to move to Hexham, Northumberland, which was considered to be a safe distance from the coast.

John then began to work in the Moscardini family business at Stanley, helping to run Uncle Federigo's billiard hall. Early in 1943 he volunteered to serve in the British Navy. His application for the Navy was rejected on the grounds of his Italian parentage. He was very upset by this decision and he became very bitter towards the authorities.

When he was eventually conscripted into the British Armed Forces, he at first attempted to register as a conscientious objector. His objections were overruled and he was posted into the Pioneer Corps as a non-combatant.

After Italy capitulated in September 1943, John reckoned that there was no longer any reason for him to be a non-combatant and he volunteered to serve in the Italian theatre. This way he reckoned he might be able to visit Sommocolonia to see Mother, Aldo and me. However, true to the 'logical bureaucratic' mind of the Army authorities he found himself posted to the Far East. There he served in the Royal Artillery until the end of the war. He eventually ended up being promoted to sergeant.

The business premises in Bedlington Station were soon to be commandeered by the authorities and opened as a 'British Restaurant'. In 1940, the Ministry of Food had encouraged the setting up of industrial canteens and lent money to local authorities to start British Restaurants for the benefit of the public.

The local authorities thus ran the British Restaurants and they were set up in a variety of premises such as schools and church halls. These restaurants provided useful supplements to the meagre wartime rations at a very reasonable price. The food in the British Restaurants however was very basic and completely unimaginative and they were unable to withstand the competition when commercial cafeterias started to trade again at the end of the war.

British Restaurants finally began to disband soon after the end of hostilities in Europe and they were eventually wound up completely in 1946. I remember frequenting a British Restaurant when I was attending school in Newcastle-upon-Tyne in the late spring of 1946. The meals were very cheap but completely uninspiring.

Then, Fenwicks, the famous Department store in Northumberland Street, opened a new cafeteria. We students immediately deserted the British Restaurant and began to flock to Fenwick's cafeteria. We did not mind standing in a long queue in order to get a really tasty hot meal.

Mother was by now getting quite big carrying my little brother. At the beginning of September off she went to the local hospital in Barga to give birth.

My aunt Dora and my grandmother Adele (née Passerotti) had arranged that I should go and stay with the Passerotti family whilst my mother was in hospital. The Passerottis were one of the largest families in the village and they lived in a fairly big three-storey house only a couple of minutes walk away.

The bedrooms were on the third floor and I was allocated a small guestroom right at one end of the house. In order to get to this room I had to walk through two other bedrooms.

That first night when I was walking along to my bedroom I began to think that something was wrong with my sight for I could see little black spots dancing before my eyes. I then realised, to my horror, that there was nothing wrong with my eyes; those spots were fleas, scores of them.

Well I just had to tolerate it, for, after all, the Passerotti family had been very kind by agreeing to look after me. Mother did not stay very long in the hospital. Nevertheless, it was with great delight that I heard the news that she would soon be coming home from hospital. My gladness at her return was rendered even more joyful by the fact that she had brought back home with her a lovely little baby brother.

He was christened Aldo, which was rather strange, because children, particularly boys, were usually named after forefathers. In fact my brother John had been christened Giovanni after our maternal grandfather and I had been christened Bonafede after our paternal grandfather. Nevertheless we all agreed that Aldo was a lovely name.

By strange coincidence my aunt Rosina, my father's youngest sister, was also expecting that year. She went down to the hospital in Barga in October and gave birth to twin girls, *Ilda* and *Maria*. Her husband *Fiore* was a bit of a card. On hearing the news of the twins he declared: "If I had known they were going to give her **two** babies I certainly wouldn't have allowed her to go to the hospital!"

Chapter 4

The earliest memory that I have of my childhood is of this very hospital in Barga. In 1934, at the age of three my mother took me over to Italy to have my tonsils removed. My parents erroneously believed that the medical treatment in Italy would be best. The hospital in Barga, called *San Francesco,* was staffed by a nursing order of nuns. Mother duly took me down to the hospital to have the tonsillectomy.

At the hospital *San Francesco* there was no attempt to make me feel at ease before the operation. I was led to an operating room and just plonked on a rather high chair. The operation was to take place without anaesthetic. I recall that the room had a very bare look about it, as did the whole hospital. This was not exactly a reassuring sight to a frightened young child.

The surgeon then tried to insert a long instrument into my mouth. I was so frightened that I instinctively jumped off the chair. A nun was standing guard in the doorway. She had a stern impassive look on her face and her demeanour was cold and unfriendly. I then darted through the legs of the matronly nursing sister on guard in the doorway and began to run along the corridor shouting: "Leave me alone, leave me alone." Several people came running after me, caught me and dragged me, screaming, back to the operating room.

Without even trying to pacify me, they immediately placed me back on the chair where two people held me down very firmly, whilst a third person forcibly held my mouth open. The surgeon then proceeded with the operation. This was undoubtedly the most terrifying incident in my life, which I remember so vividly even to this day.

I was told years later that a traumatic experience of this kind could have been sufficient to kill a young child. I was certainly badly affected by this uncivilised incident. For years afterwards I would not even consider going near a hospital.

When I was recounting this experience several years later to an acquaintance, Mr Fazzi, from Glasgow, I learnt that he had also had a similar experience. As a child his parents had taken him over to Italy to have his tonsils removed. At that very same hospital in Barga they had proceeded to operate on him in the same manner without any anaesthetic. This barbaric treatment was obviously standard procedure in Italy in the early 1930s.

That first summer in Sommocolonia was a very difficult one for me. The children of the village would not play with me and I felt very much alone and really unhappy. Whenever I tried to join them they would have nothing to do with me and would say: *"Va a casa* (go home) *Inglesaccio bastardo".* The suffix '-accio' has a pejorative meaning in Italian and I think one can guess the rest.

I kept trying to associate with the other children but they would continually reject me and many was the time that I ran home in tears. Being forced in this manner to rely on my own devices I had to try and amuse myself as best possible. I had no toys but I had a small tin full of out of date Italian coins and several other foreign coins in small denominations. I would spend many hours alone in my bedroom and play war games with these coins. The coins were the soldiers and I never tired of these imaginary battles where the British troops would always end up winning.

The only person who did not mind playing with me was Peppe Cecchini, a boy who was approximately eighteen months younger than me. He was in fact our next door neighbour who lived only a few yards away.

Peppe was renowned as being a bit of a *matterello* (daft). One day while we were wandering about in the chestnut woods, Peppe spotted a snake. He turned to me and said:

" Come on find a stick and let's get that snake." The snake ran off and went to ground at the base of a large tree trunk.

I immediately felt relieved at this because I was not really fond of snakes and thankfully that would be the end of the matter.

But Peppe was not going to let it rest. He proceeded to dig around with his stick in the tree trunk until the snake, which had by this time become very angry, suddenly shot out of its hiding hole and came rushing headlong in my direction. I took one look and ran off faster than I had ever done before.

I kept on running and the snake just continued to come after me. I could not believe that a snake was capable of slithering along the ground so fast. After what seemed like an eternity I finally managed to outpace the snake and reach the safety of a large clearing.

Peppe was by now laughing his head off. When I confided to him that I had had a real fear of dying, he just casually said: "You needn't have worried. It was only a non-venomous *serpone*. At worst you would have just received a lashing from its tail." This did not reassure me in the least. On the contrary it resulted in me developing an even more deep-rooted fear of snakes, which I have not managed to shed even to this day.

On another occasion that summer I had gone to the southernmost edge of the village in search of someone to play with. In the end house there lived a family known as the *Cascianella* family. They had three children fairly close to my age but they did not express much desire for my company. On the contrary, one of the children set their dog, a large Alsatian, onto me.

This enormous dog suddenly bounded towards me and before I realised what was happening, it had bitten me on the back of my leg. This caused quite a commotion and Mr Cascianella came out to see what was happening. When he saw what had occurred he was very apologetic and he remonstrated very severely with his children.

He then proceeded to clean my wound with hydrogen peroxide and treat it with surgical spirit. Fortunately it was only a light surface wound but it nevertheless made a big impression on me for it left me with a life-long fear of dogs. After that I ventured down to that part of the village very rarely.

When I mentioned this incident to Peppe, he delighted in telling me the story of the village priest and his dog. Apparently the priest was very fond of dogs and some years before the war he had also kept a large Alsatian. They say that Alsatian dogs have wolf blood in them and are liable to arbitrarily revert to a feral nature.

One day this Alsatian suddenly turned on its master and bit him very severely on one leg. In fact he had great difficulty releasing himself. The dog was immediately put down but meanwhile the priest's leg wound had become very badly infected.

In those pre-war days there were very few medicines for infected bites. The priest was therefore advised to cauterise the wound, a considerably painful method of treatment. It transpired that he ended up cauterising his wound with a red-hot poker each day for several weeks. When the wound finally began to heal he vowed that he would never keep another dog. This 'reassuring' story made me quite apprehensive. Fortunately my wound was very superficial. I certainly would not have relished the 'red-hot poker treatment'!

The village boys continued to boycott me all summer long and make fun of me whenever I tried to join them. Mother attempted to remonstrate with them and even confronted some of their parents but this tended to make matters worse because such childhood difficulties have to be sorted out by the person concerned.

When I started school in late September I was in daily contact with the other children. It was during one of their teasing and bullying bouts after school that I finally managed to resolve the matter.

One day, I had just got to the end of my tether. I could not stand it any longer. I therefore challenged one of my coevals to a fight. Fortunately, I won this fight and for some inexplicable reason most of the boys began to accept me and even started to respect me. For I was no longer the snivelling little wimp who continually ran off home crying to his mother.

I still had to put up with some bullying from one or two of the older boys, but the bullying got gradually less and less until it eventually petered out completely. Incidentally the boy I thrashed became quite a good friend of mine.

In the autumn I started school in the *Quarta Elementare* (year 4 of primary school) in the new village school which had just been opened the previous year. At that time the compulsory school attendance age in Italy was between the ages of six and eleven. One of the good things that had resulted from the Fascist regime was that Mussolini had tried to ensure that every child of compulsory school age would be provided with a school place.

And so many new primary schools were built throughout Italy. I remember the school being built in Sommocolonia. When I went over with mother for my usual summer holiday in 1938, the school was still under construction. I would often wander up to the building site with other children to watch the builders at work. I particularly recall that we were constantly being warned by the workmen to take great care and stay well clear of the lime pits.

Prior to the opening of the new state-of-the-art school, lessons in the village would take place in a large room in *Benito's* house at *Monte*. *Benito*, who was the same age as me, also had the surname Moscardini. He was not a close relative but I am sure that if one went back some generations he would most probably have been related to me.

The schoolmistress was called Signora Ersilia Casciani. Lessons were conducted on a shift basis. Signora Casciani would take classes four and five in the morning, and classes one, two and three in the afternoon.

In 1937, we had taken our customary summer holiday rather late. We went over at the beginning of September and remained in Sommocolonia until the end of October.

When school started at the end of September, I was encouraged to go along. I particularly remember that time because Signora Casciani was reading the story of Pinocchio. Her readings would be punctuated with appropriate facial gestures and gesticulations.

All the children sat enthralled and laughed and cheered at various times. Although I could not understand a word, I was spellbound and somewhat envious that I could not participate in the sheer joy and delight of the other children. My interest was aroused however, and, as

I grew older, Pinocchio became one of my favourite children's books, which I read over and over many times.

For some reason I was not particularly keen on going to Italy that year. In fact I remember stating to my parents that I categorically did not want to go. Father was quite insistent, wanting to know the reason why. I believe I mentioned something to the effect that I could enjoy myself better in England. Then Father replied: "Just think. You are going over to see *Nonno* and he is eagerly looking forward to your visit".

At this I thought: "Great, I will be able to play with *Nonno*". When I got to Sommocolonia I was very disappointed to discover that *Nonno* was not really a playmate. On the contrary he was an old man, my grandfather.

Chapter 5

My paternal grandfather, Bonafede, had travelled quite extensively abroad. His first journey was in 1877 when, at the young age of seventeen, he went to Derby to work for a Mr Biagiotti as a *figurinaio*, a door to door salesman of religious statuettes.

In 1879 he had to register for military service and this necessitated him returning home to Italy. Later that same year he journeyed back to England, this time to London. After working here for nearly two years as a *figurinaio* he was obliged, in 1882, to report to the Italian military authorities in Florence for a three-month compulsory period of military service.

Upon completion of his military service he travelled to Baltimore in the United States where he set up in partnership with the same Mr Biagiotti, managing a small firm of statuette salesmen. He spent three years in America in charge of several Italian *figurinai*. In this manner he managed to save a considerable sum of money and he returned to his father's family in Sommocolonia for a break of about six months. It was during this period that he purchased a house in the village, which was to become the Moscardini paternal family home.

He made yet another trip to the States, this time to Philadelphia. After returning to Italy to get married to his childhood sweetheart, Maria Marchetti, he set off again in 1890 for Liverpool in England. His final journey in the UK was to Glasgow in Scotland where he set up in business selling ice cream, confectionery and tobacco products. It was at this juncture that he sent for his two younger brothers Ferruccio and Sabatino to come and work with him.

Nonno Bonafede was a very religious man of high moral standards. He did not squander his money but was an assiduous saver. With his earnings he was able to purchase not only the house but also several plots of land and woodlands during his many return visits to his native village. It's astounding to think how far he travelled considering the fact that, in those days, long journeys overseas were normally undertaken only once in one's lifetime.

His last business enterprise was in Glasgow, where, along with his two brothers he established a very profitable bakery specialising in Italian bread. He supplied this bread on a daily basis to the very large Italian community in the city of Glasgow at that time.

He even bought a horse-drawn vehicle for the daily deliveries of bread. In 1895, whilst on the bread round, his brother Ferruccio suffered a terrible accident with the horse. On trying to ascertain the reason for a limp, which the horse had suddenly developed, he sustained a very severe kick in the head, which resulted in his early death.

Nonno Bonafede had kept a rather sketchy diary of the period of his travels abroad and his account of his brother Ferruccio's death is so poignant that it brought tears to my eyes when I first read it.

In translating the following extract from his handwritten diary, I have tried to keep to the spirit of the language of the original account in Italian:

'*Poor Ferruccio, he would insist on going out with the horse and cart. To this day, I still grieve about that fatal date. On 5 May 1895, off he went, in the pink of health, for the first time on his own, on an errand for Mr P Nardini. It would have been better if he had not gone. He left at 0700. At 1150 I saw the horse and cart in front of the shop. I said to my friend Gianpiero: "my brother's returned for lunch."*

I went over to look. A man from Barga had brought the horse back. He said that my brother had fallen from the cart and hurt his head. I asked him where he was. "At the police station", he replied. I suddenly went all cold. I caught the tram. I think I only travelled a short distance, and then I ran to the police station.

I found him at the police station, all covered in blood and unable to speak. Crying, I immediately took him in my arms. I carried him home without saying a word. Then I sent for the doctor. He said that the horse had kicked my brother in the head and that there was no hope. At 1500 he passed over into the next world.

Oh dearest brother Ferruccio, you could have at least spoken something to me! What a horrendous tragedy for me that took away my dear brother in the space of a day! I have shed many tears for you and I am still crying three years later when I write this.

The whole Italian community in Glasgow mourned him. The Italian "Società di Mutuo Soccorso" took charge of matters. There followed a grand funeral the likes of which had never been organised for any Italian in Glasgow. He was accompanied to the cemetery by 12 carriages.

Dario Nardini, the Secretary of the "Società di Mutuo Soccorso" gave a fine speech at the graveside, a copy of which I have attached. Goodbye once again my dear Ferruccio. I shall always remember you in this diary.'

Bonafede was so distressed by this tragic accident that he decided to sell all his business interests and return to his native Sommocolonia, where he remained until his own death in 1939.

In those days most of the Italian men who went abroad to seek their fortune would invariably leave their wives behind. *Nonno* Bonafede had fathered six children during his many return visits to his native village: three boys and three girls. Speranza was the eldest. Then came Federigo, Giuseppe (my father), Argene, Mansueto and Rosina.

Of the six children four of them emigrated in order to seek a better way of life. Speranza went to America, and the three boys, Federigo, Giuseppe and Mansueto went to Tyneside in northeast England. Argene and Rosina remained in Sommocolonia for it was not usual for girls to emigrate unless called over by relatives.

My aunt Speranza voyaged to America by pure chance. My uncle Federigo had yearned to go to America and he had even purchased a ticket for the United States. His older sister Speranza accompanied him to Genova where he was to catch the ship.

When Federigo came to board the liner bound for America he was refused permission because he was not old enough. On the spur of the moment, Speranza decided that it would be a shame to waste the ticket and off she went to America in Federigo's place.

Whilst in Sommocolonia, Speranza had fallen in love with a young man of the village called Omero. They had become engaged and Omero had gone to America to seek his fortune, intending to send for his fiancée as soon as he had earned and saved sufficient money. Speranza would eventually have gone to America at any rate. This way she was able to go there sooner and they were able to get married earlier than they expected.

Costante, the husband of my aunt Argene, also went over to America to seek his fortune and avoid doing his military service. He went to work for his older brother Giuseppe Marchetti. Costante returned twice to his native village and it was during these visits that he fathered his two daughters, Gina and Maria.

He would send money back from time to time but he was unable to do this when America entered the war. It was therefore fortunate that Argene was able to enjoy the fruits of a smallholding and a sizeable tract of chestnut woodlands, which *Nonno* Bonafede had purchased. Costante lived most of his life in America, and I never really got to meet him. I am told that he was a real dapper chap and he had quite an eye for the ladies.

Another so-called grass widow in the village was a woman called Catera. Her husband Barbetta had also gone to America. On his visits back to the village he had fathered four children: Dante, Anna, Mario and Leda. Catera had a very hard time of it during the war because she had no land and had to bring up four growing children solely on the meagre rations of the time.

Catera was very strict with her children and thus had no difficulty in keeping them under control. If she needed to talk to any of them she would whistle. She had a very loud whistle, which could be heard from one end of the village to the other. Whenever her children heard their mother whistling for them they would immediately abandon whatever they were doing and rush straight back home.

My Aunt Rosina married a local man called Fioravante (Fiore) Cecchini. Their family lived with *Nonna* Maria in the paternal home at *Monte*. They had a sizeable tract of land called *Colto*, which incorporated several fields and surrounding chestnut woodlands. They also looked after another chestnut woodland nearer the village. All these lands were quite sufficient to keep Rosina, Fiore and the whole family busy all year round. Besides the twins, Ilda and Maria, Rosina had two older children, Renzo and Vito, both boys.

The new village primary school was a building consisting of two enormously large classrooms with very high ceilings. In fact they tended to resemble gymnasiums. There were also several storerooms and cupboards and cubbyholes.

Signora Casciani now had an assistant. The fact that the new school had two classrooms and two teachers meant that all the pupils could be taught in one morning session lasting from eight am to one pm. This was welcomed by everyone because it meant that in the afternoon all the children could help their families with the work in the fields and woodlands. The new assistant taught the first three years and Signora Casciani tutored years four and five.

One particular thing about my schooling that I shall not forget was the fact that, every morning, when the schoolmistress first came into the classroom we all had to stand up, make the fascist salute and shout: *"Viva il Duce"*.

This had been decreed by the Duce himself. Another decree of the fascist era was that every young person automatically became a member of the Italian fascist youth organisation.

In 1926, the Italian fascist party had instituted the '*Opera Nazionale Balilla*' which was a youth organisation catering for everyone up to the age of twenty-one. In 1928 all non-fascist youth organisations in Italy were declared illegal. And so all children and youths were automatically enrolled into the fascist system. The various designations for boys and girls were as follows:

Boys:
6 to 7 years   - Figlio della Lupa
8 to 12 years   - Balilla

13 to 17 years - Avanguardista
18 to 21 years - Giovane Fascista

Girls:
6 to 7 years   - Figlia della Lupa
8 to 12 years   - Piccola Italiana
13 to 17 years - Giovane Italiana
18 to 21 years - Giovane Fascista

The Fascist motto was: *Credere* (Believe), *Ubbidire* (Obey), e *Combattere* (Fight).

Thus I automatically became a Balilla.

Mussolini had also decreed that all young people had to undertake *ginnastica* (PE) on Saturday afternoons. In the isolated little mountain village nobody insisted on this compulsory PE. Besides, the children had more pressing activities to undertake on Saturdays: helping their parents in the fields and woodlands. In the same way they were not forced to wear the prescribed uniform, although some of the boys did in fact wear a cap and a scarf.

The terms *figlio/figlia della Lupa* (son/daughter of the she-wolf) referred to the famous legend of the orphaned twins Romulus and Remus, who, after being suckled by a she-wolf, grew up to found the city of Rome.

Balilla was a boy who lived in Genova in the eighteenth century. At that time the Genoese Republic was under the domination of the Austro-Hungarian Empire. The Genoese people were not very happy with this situation and, in 1746, during one of the many verbal confrontations between the citizens of the city and the foreign occupiers, Balilla threw a stone at the troops.

This action by a little boy proved to be the catalyst, which galvanised the inhabitants into action. They then turned on the foreign troops and succeeded in liberating the city from the foreign yoke. Balilla of course was hailed as a national hero.

All the school textbooks were interspersed with paragraphs, verses and slogans praising the Fascist Regime and delineating all the great things that *Il Duce* had done for *La Patria* (the Motherland). These were usually to be found in the corner of a page.

Even around the village there were several rectangular marble plaques praising *Il Duce* and citing various other items of Fascist propaganda. These plaques would normally be placed in prominent spots, affixed to houses.

The first visible effect of Italy entering the war was that all the metal railings around the village were commandeered and cut down by the authorities to aid the Italian war effort.

Mussolini also made an impassioned appeal to the patriotic sentiments of all female citizens to donate their gold rings to aid *La Patria* in its fight against 'British Imperialism'. As a consequence many Italian housewives surrendered their gold wedding rings to the Fascist State.

Nonno Bonafede's family, Circa 1909. From left to right.
Back row: Speranza, Nonna Maria, Argene, Giuseppe (dad) &
Federigo. Front row: Rosina, Nonno Bonafede & Mansueto.

Speranza Moscardini & husband Omero Bertagna.

Federigo Moscardini & wife Fernanda.

Mansueto Moscardini.

Aunt Argene & her two daughters, Gina & Maria.

Costante Marchetti, Argene's husband.

Aunt Rosina & husband Fioravante Cecchini. Their 4 children left to right: Vito, Maria, Ilda & Renzo.

Chapter 6

That first winter struck me as being a particularly cold one but when I think back on this it was probably due to the house we were living in.

The house was situated at *Monticino* on the northern edge of the village just before arriving at the new school. The house belonged to the extended Passerotti family and because of this my grandmother Adele had the right to live in it.

It was really a very small dwelling, consisting of four rooms, two up and two down. Downstairs there was a reasonably sized kitchen cum living room and a small sitting room (or parlour) which was hardly ever used. In fact during the four years we lived there I doubt whether it was used more than a dozen times.

A wooden staircase at one end of the kitchen led up to the two upstairs bedrooms, which roughly corresponded in size to the two downstairs rooms. At the top of the stairs there was a toilet with what can only be described as "State-of-the-Ark" sanitation.

This was merely a sort of garderobe: the toilet itself was a wooden bench with a hole in the centre. A wooden lid with a handle covered the hole like a plug. All the waste products would go down a wooden chute and end up in the cellar. Not quite as disgusting as the toilet described in Boccaccio's tale "Andreuccio da Perugia", but nevertheless extremely primitive.

There was no cesspit and the stench of this toilet was absolutely unbearable especially in the heat of the summer. We ensured that the door was always well closed and the window open. Consequently, in the summer, it was always buzzing with flies.

This room was so small that there was barely enough space for a person to sit down and close the door. No way was I going to use this primitive 'loo' and during the whole of my stay in Sommocolonia I invariably went out into the woods or the fields for my calls of nature.

The waste products in the basement would be cleared away every two to three years. I remember when this was done one year. The scene was absolutely indescribable and how the labourer could bring himself to carry out such a task I do not know. Normally I was always very interested in whatever work went on. On this occasion I left very early for I was absolutely disgusted with the overpowering stench of the human ordure.

The house had no land attached to it. On the west it abutted the road and on the east it overlooked a large field and a cowshed. This stable was the cause of many flies in the summer. The windows downstairs looked out over this field and the cowshed.

In the summer, it would get very hot indoors. In the living room we could open the front door for fresh air but the only means of cooling down the sitting room was opening the window. If we did this, the room would be swarming with flies within minutes. We often had to spray the room with fly killer.

There were no aerosols in those days. The fly spray consisted of a short cylindrical metal container, which we would fill with a fly killer liquid called 'Flit'. By using the hand pump attached to the container we could spray liquid into the air. The fly spray was very effective because within about ten minutes the floor of the room would be covered in dead flies. But one only had to open the window and in no time it would be full of flies again.

At the front, just outside the entrance door to the house, there was a very small cemented triangular stretch of ground barely large enough for a couple of chairs and a small table.

Our family income was very limited. Grandmother Adele had a sum of money in a deposit account in an Italian bank but these funds would not last forever. Mother and Aunt Dora had to try and supplement our meagre income by going out to work. That first autumn and winter Mother would go out into the woods looking for wood and kindling for the fire. Dora tried to get a cleaning job but this meant going down to Barga and she was only able to get the occasional day or two.

Grandmother Adele was a very lovable person. Her close presence was a constant source of comfort to me. Whenever she spoke it was always in a gentle tone of voice and she never shouted or lost her temper. She was undoubtedly my favourite 'granny'. She had a very majestic sort of demeanour and, unlike the older women in the village, she never wore black.

She looked after baby Aldo during the day and I remember her singing *La Ninna Nanna* (a lullaby) while rocking the cradle and getting him to sleep. Aldo was swathed in swaddling clothes for the first few months. In fact he was bandaged very tightly from his neck to his feet. The theory was that a newborn baby had to be tightly wrapped to prevent him from harming his delicate bones. This illustrates how primitive life was, up in those mountains, only sixty odd years ago.

Mother would often come home laden with faggots of wood and sometimes she would be carrying wood for other people. She would of course be recompensed for this, but in kind, not in money. This might consist of flour, olive oil, fresh vegetables, dried borlotti beans, chestnut flour or other food. It was a welcome bounty for we were very grateful for anything that came our way.

After about a year and several applications to the relevant authorities, Mother, Aunt Dora and Grandmother Adele were each granted a small *sussidio* (a kind of pension) by the Italian government. This was because their husbands were interned in England as enemy aliens. Although it was only a token monthly sum every little helped.

In the kitchen there was a very large open fireplace and during the winter a wood fire would be continually burning in the hearth. From the chimney hung an adjustable metal chain with a hook on the end for hanging pots and cauldrons above the fire.

The major cooking was done over this wooden fire, which also acted as the only means of heating the room. It was in actual fact a very inefficient form of heating for in the winter your front could be roasting whereas your back was chilled by the ice-cold draught blowing in through the front door.

Unfortunately, the door was north facing. This meant that on cold winter days and evenings an arctic wind would literally whistle in through this ill-fitting door. Cooking a main meal over the fire was usually a very arduous task. In the summer it was doubly tiresome because of the enormous heat.

By the fire would be a *soffione* which served as a sort of bellows to rekindle the fire. This consisted of a long metal tube with a hole in the middle and one would blow very hard down the tube to get the fire going again. Sometimes when the wood was still green or damp the kitchen would fill with smoke necessitating opening the door and window to clear the room. The firewood was usually chestnut, not an ideal wood for burning. The pots and cauldrons were all made of copper.

Two small charcoal ovens, which had been built in one corner of the kitchen, provided a subsidiary form of cooking. These were just for small matters such as making some soup, boiling a saucepan of water or heating milk and coffee for breakfast.

In one corner of the kitchen/living room was *la conca del bucato*, a large terracotta pot standing about two to three feet tall for the *bucato*, the laundry. All the sheets, pillowcases and towels were white and made of linen.

Down at *Rio*, the nearest river, the villagers had diverted part of the flow of water to irrigate a wide flat area. Here they grew flax. When the flax rushes were ready they would be cut and steeped for a few days in order to make it easier to remove the outer bark, which was to be used for the fibre. This bark would eventually be carded and spun and would be used to weave sheets, pillowcases and towels.

It was the custom that girls started amassing linen for their bottom drawer right from an early age. All this *biancheria* (white linen) would be their dowry. It was not unusual for a young bride to have collected twenty to thirty pairs of sheets and pillowcases and towels before her marriage. This dowry would probably last the young bride the whole of her life.

There were several women in Barga who had a loom in the house and would weave white goods for a reasonable sum. I remember one day going along with Aunt Dora to visit her mother in law. I was astonished when I entered to find her sitting at a loom busily weaving a blanket. I stood there absolutely fascinated as I watched her propelling by hand the shuttle back and forth at considerable speed.

The large terracotta pot used for the *bucato* was normally cemented into a corner. The interior was glazed to render it non-porous and it had a tap with a spout near the bottom. The system for doing the *bucato* was as follows: all the dirty linen would be folded and neatly placed in layers in the pot up to about four inches from the brim. On top would be placed an old sheet to protect the good linen. This old sheet would then be covered with a layer of white wood ash about two inches thick.

A large cauldron would be hung over the wood fire, which would be filled with water. When the water was very hot the housewife would scoop out a quantity of hot water in a copper ladle and pour it over the wood ash. The wood ash apparently acted as a natural form of bleach.

The water would slowly filter through the linen until it poured out at the bottom where it was collected in another receptacle. Then this water would be replaced into the cauldron to be heated again.

Meanwhile, a fresh lot of hot water would be poured over the wood ash and the whole process would be repeated ad infinitum. Normally, the *bucato* would be started first thing in the morning and it would last all day. Inevitably it was a very hot and tedious task and it was done very infrequently.

The following day the terracotta pot would be emptied and the linen placed into baskets and taken down to the communal wash place. At the wash place there were two large concrete tubs, with a cold water tap. Here, the housewife would spend hours rinsing the laundry.

The wash tubs were a real boon because, prior to their erection, the housewives would have had to carry the laundry all the way down to *Rio*, the nearest river, a considerable journey there and back.

After the linen had been thoroughly rinsed through, it would be hung out to dry. The ironing would be done with an enormous heavy iron. In the base of this iron there was a deep space for hot embers, to make the iron hot enough for pressing.

Very few of the houses in the village had running water and those that did only had a cold tap connected directly to the mains. In this respect we were lucky because we had running cold water in the kitchen. This meant a tap above the kitchen sink.

A large public fountain had been installed in the village square for the benefit of the inhabitants. The water for the village came straight from a mountain spring and the fountain gushed forth continually day and night all year round. In the summer the water was lovely and cool and even those people with water in their houses would often go and fill a container from the public fountain in order to drink some nice cool fresh water.

Those houses, which were not connected to the mains, had to collect their water from the fountain in the village *piazza*. They would fill their buckets and pots and pans and carry them all the way back home.

They stored the drinking water in a copper container. Inside this container would be a copper ladle and anyone who wished to have a drink would just lift this ladle to their mouths and drink. People seldom bothered to wipe this ladle but on thinking back I cannot recall anybody catching any disease by drinking from a ladle.

One house in the village was only connected up to the mains water supply as late as 1995. I gather that the housewife was absolutely delighted. At last she could indulge in the pleasure of owning a washing machine, undoubtedly the greatest labour saving household device ever invented.

One of the men in the village, called Bruno, was a bit of a practical joker. Along with most of the other men he never shaved from one weekend to the next. Consequently he always sported rough stubble on his face. He loved grabbing little boys and rubbing his beard on their tender faces. To him this may have seemed hilarious but it could be quite painful.

One day, he asked me to go along to the village *bottega* and buy five *centesimi* (cents) of *grugno pesto*. The word *pesto* meant ground, crushed, but what I didn't know was that *grugno* was a dialect word meaning face.

As I entered the *bottega* a little bell rang and the shopkeeper came into the shop area from the adjoining room. He asked me what I wanted. I said: "Bruno has sent me for 5 *centesimi* of *grugno pesto*. And can you please add it to his bill". With a big grin the shopkeeper said: "Come here", then he grabbed me and proceeded to screw his knuckles into my face. He didn't really hurt because he did it quite gently.

The *bottega* was situated in the *piazza*, the village square, It was the only retail shop in the village. It consisted of a *Sali e Tabacchi* and a general grocery store. It also sold various kinds of household articles that might be needed.

Salt and tobacco products were a state monopoly in those days. The government strictly controlled retail outlets for the sale of salt, matches and tobacco products. To have a *Sali e Tabacchi* licence meant that you were assured of a very comfortable living.

These licences were usually granted to *Mutilati di Guerra* (disabled ex-servicemen) or other people for services to their country. In the cities this licence meant that you would be quite well off. And even in small villages like Sommocolonia it guaranteed quite a reasonable living.

Sali e Tabacchi outlets still exist in Italy today at the beginning of the twenty-first century. And so you have the ridiculous anachronistic anomaly that, although the sale of salt has been deregulated and tobacco products are now more widely available, you can't buy matches in a grocery shop or supermarket. You must still go to a licensed *Sali e Tabacchi* outlet to purchase a box of matches.

The proprietor of the shop was called Netto. He would go down to Barga every weekday morning to collect fresh bread and any other items that were needed. The shop was very small and not suitable for large stocks of groceries. Therefore many items were not stocked but could be purchased by ordering them the day before.

There was always a very distinctive smell to the *bottega*. This was from the *baccalà*, (dried salted cod) that was hanging from the ceiling and the barrel of salted sardines that were sold by the *etto* (hectogram).

The road from Barga to Sommocolonia was a normal tarmac road as far as Ponte di Catagnana. From there it was a climb all the way by means of a mule track. It was a very winding road, which snaked backwards and forwards up the mountain.

It was a gently sloping road but the last half-kilometre or so was quite steep. Although it was paved in local stones it was not wide enough for vehicular traffic. Also anything heavy would probably have damaged the surface of the road.

Netto had a donkey, which he loaded with two long fluted basket type panniers. On the return journey from Barga these panniers would usually be filled to the brim. By midday there would be a sizeable group of people waiting in the *piazza* for Netto to return with fresh bread. On the last steep stretch Netto was in the habit of holding on to the donkey's tail to help him up that most difficult part.

The story goes that this donkey suffered terribly with wind and often this wind would be blown straight into Netto's face. One day Netto had had enough of this and he decided to plug the donkey's rectum with a large cork.

Well this did not stop the donkey's flatulence; on the contrary its stomach began to swell and swell until eventually the pressure built up so much that it propelled the cork out with considerable speed and force. The cork hit Netto right in the middle of the forehead and knocked him out. Netto never tried to plug the donkey again.

Late October that year, I had terrible toothache and Mother took me down to the dentist in Barga. He took one look at me, said: "Come here scotchy" in broken English, and plonked me on a chair. I was rather taken aback by him calling me 'scotchy' and I could not understand the reason why.

It wasn't till many years later, well after the end of the war, that I understood his meaning. Most of the Italians who had emigrated from the Barga region had gone to Scotland and this dentist had erroneously assumed that every Anglo-Italian coming from the UK originated from Scotland. The dentist then proceeded to extract my tooth without anaesthetic. The pain is still vivid in my memory and I was never very keen to pay another visit to this dentist.

On the feast of the Epiphany, it was the custom for children to go around and sing *La Befana* in the same way as people go carol singing at Christmas in the UK. Normally children would go around in groups of three or four. However, I could not find anyone who would come with me and I was really very upset.

My grandmother Adele kept insisting that I should go along to the priest's house on my own to sing *La Befana*. She said that, as her sister Palmira was the priest's housekeeper, I would be sure of a good welcome.

After a lot of persuasion, I mustered up enough courage and set off with a basket. I would hate to think what my singing must have sounded like. I had barely started to sing *La Befana*, when suddenly the door was opened. There stood Palmira beaming from ear to ear. She had obviously been forewarned about my visit. Before I knew what was happening she proceeded to fill my basket with all kinds of cakes and other goodies.

The priest was called Don Fredianelli. He was a tall lanky fellow and Fernandel's portrayal of Don Camillo in the post-war films reminded me very much of Don Fredianelli. The priest was in fact quite well off, despite the meagre rationing of the time. Most of the parishioners still paid a kind of tithes to their parish priest. This consisted of flour, oil, wine, and other basic products from their smallholdings.

The villagers were all very poor in monetary terms and the weekly collections would usually amount to only a few coppers. Nevertheless the parish priest lived well with all those contributions in kind. He never wanted for food or drink and he was renowned for his enormous capacity for eating and drinking.

It was reputed that he could down a whole bottle of local wine in one go without even pausing for breath. Despite this gargantuan capacity for food and drink he was not fat. He must have been full of nervous energy to be able to expend this rather large calorific intake.

He was a very demonstrative and outgoing person. I remember one particular idiosyncrasy of his. He had this habit of blowing his nose very noisily. He would often pause in the middle of his sermon at mass and take several minutes over this nasal operation.

On the other hand he was very conscientious about carrying out his pastoral duties. Even on the coldest winter mornings when the snow was several inches deep he would set off along a narrow mountain path to say mass at 7am in one of the scattered hamlets of the parish several kilometres away. I do not remember him ever being prevented by the weather from going to say mass.

I recall sitting down one year with a couple of other boys and we began to make a rough list of all the people who lived in the village. We reckoned that there were just fewer than three hundred souls in the village itself. The parish of Sommocolonia however embraced several small hamlets, including Catagnana, and many scattered cottages in the surrounding hills.

In all just over four hundred inhabitants had been registered in a recent census shortly prior to the outbreak of war. So we reckoned that our spontaneous 'mini-census' was more or less accurate.

The life of the village centred around the church calendar. All the families would work hard all week and rest on Sundays. The mechanical clock in the *campanile* next to the church rang the hours day and night. It would strike one to six, so that, five strokes denoted either five o'clock or eleven o'clock, and three strokes denoted three o'clock or nine o'clock and so on. The hammer of the clock striking against the bell could be heard for miles around. This was the only way that the villagers could tell the exact time (on the hour) because none of them could afford to own a watch.

At midday, the *Angelus* bell would be rung for several minutes. This bell also served to inform the peasants labouring in the fields and woodlands that it was time for lunch.

In the *campanile* were three bells: *la piccola*, the small bell, *la mezzana*, the middle-sized bell, and *la grossa*, the big bell. On Sundays and Holy days of obligation there would always be three peals of three bells each lasting about six to seven minutes. The first peal would be rung forty-five minutes before the start of mass, the second peal thirty minutes before mass and the last peal fifteen minutes before. Then, two or three minutes before the start of the service, *la campanella*, a very small bell would be rung to warn the congregation that mass was about to begin. On weekdays there would be only one peal of two bells, *la piccola e la mezzana* thirty minutes before the start of the service.

Generally, Sunday was a day of rest and no work would be done in the fields.   The only work normally undertaken on Sundays was milking cows and feeding any animals. However, at harvest time, when there was a great urgency to ensure that the harvest was safely gathered in, they would relax this rule.

Most families had a cow. Those families who did not possess a cow could buy milk by the cupful. It would be raw milk and it had to be boiled. The milk from one cow however was not sufficient in itself to produce enough volume for cheese making so various families would band together into a kind of cooperative and thereby take turns to make cheese.

On winter evenings it was quite usual to go along to taste *la scotta*. This meant going along to one of the families whose turn it was for cheese making and drinking cups of hot whey. The curds of course were used for cheese making.

All the women would invariably carry goods on their head, resting on a kind of thick tea towel rolled round to form a pad. This included pails of milk and you would often see women returning from the fields in the evening carrying a pail of milk on their head.

They normally held the pail with one hand but there was one woman whose deportment was so perfect that she balanced the pail of milk on her head without any support. It was wonderful to watch her wending her way back home from the fields up and down slopes, hands on her hips, and never spilling a drop.

Chapter 7

In the spring of 1941, Don Fredianelli, announced that it was time that they held a *recita* in the village. This caused great excitement. I had no idea what a *recita* was but I soon learnt that it comprised of a kind of amateur 'gang show', in which, as many of the children as possible would be encouraged to take part. Among the items were soliloquies, recitations of poems and songs. The only item I remember is the song about the tower of Pisa, which we sang from time to time over the years.

It went:

Evviva la Torre di Pisa
Che pende, che pende e mai non vien giù
Evviva la Torre di Pisa
Che pende, che pende e mai non vien giù.

Se vuoi venir con me Maria Luisa
La guarderai ed esclamerai:
'Oh mamma mia che effetto mi fa. '

Evviva la Torre di Pisa
Che pende, che pende e mai non vien giù.

Roughly translated it meant:

Long live the Tower of Pisa
That leans and leans and never falls down.
Long live the Tower of Pisa
That leans and leans and never falls down.

If you'd like to come with me Maria Luisa
You'll look at it and then exclaim:
'Goodness me I feel ever so funny.'

Long live the Tower of Pisa
That leans and leans and never falls down.

The *recita* was held in the gardens of a house at *Monticino*, which was where Peppe, my next door neighbour on the north side, lived. It was held here for two reasons: the house had a large expanse of ground in front of it and Olinto, Peppe's father, was the only person in the village who played a musical instrument. Olinto played the piano accordion and, because of this he would always be the life and soul of the village whenever there was a festival or a dance.

The *recita* was held on a Sunday afternoon. It was a great success. Everyone participated with great enthusiasm and we all enjoyed ourselves immensely. It brought into the lives of the hard working peasants a little light relief from the everyday drudgery of their work in the fields.

At school it was soon obvious that I was streets ahead of all the other children of my age and Signora Casciani very quickly put me on to doing fifth-year maths. My main drawback was my lack of proficiency in Italian but I soon caught up before I finished my primary schooling.

It was sometime during this year that I began to smoke which was really terrible considering that I was only ten years old. All the boys in the village wanted to have a go at smoking. It was mainly through the influence of Netto's son, Piero that many of the boys began to smoke.

Cigarettes and tobacco were on ration in Italy during the war. Despite this, there was never any shortage because every adult (both male and female) aged twenty-one and over was entitled to a ration of tobacco products. As hardly any of the women in the village smoked, there were more than enough tobacco products to go around.

One or two of the older women had taken to 'snuffing' but these were so few that it made very little difference. I do remember one old lady who smoked a clay pipe. It was really amusing to watch this toothless old lady dressed in black, puffing away on a clay pipe.

Piero always had lots of cigarettes. On Sundays, when all the boys gathered together behind *Il Castello*, (the fortified castle of the Middle Ages) a quiet road just off the *piazza*, Piero would hand out one or two cigarettes which we younger boys had to take turns at having a drag.

Of course, all the boys wanted to show that they could keep up with their peers and anyone who did not even attempt to smoke was considered to be a bit 'chicken'. Another reason, which set me well on the road to smoking, was the fact that Mother smoked. She smoked *nazionali* the most popular Italian cigarette at the time.

Mother had this terrible habit of only half smoking a cigarette. She would then stub it out and replace the unsmoked half back in the packet. So I took to stealing the odd half cigarette and off I would go on my own to a quiet spot where I would secretly light up and smoke a half cigarette.

I knew that what I was doing was wrong especially as I had stolen these cigarettes but the strange thing was that these clandestine acts of mine actually stirred sexual excitement in me. This was quite delightful at first. Before long the sexual pleasure at lighting up had gone but there was no turning back. I was now well and truly hooked on the devil weed. In fact it was not till many years later, when I was well into my forties, that I managed to give up smoking completely.

I could not afford to buy any cigarettes so I had to rely on the odd half cigarette that I was able to steal from Mother. At other times I would, as all the other boys did, ask the men for their *cicca*. The *cicca* was the cigarette end, which they were about to throw away. Some people were less generous than others, because at times trying to smoke a *cicca* only resulted in burning your fingers and your lips.

One day I had a rather frightening experience whilst smoking a cigarette end that I had cadged. I was watching a group of village men who were pruning chestnut trees in the woods. During a break in their work, one of the men called Adamo started to roll a cigarette with *spuntature* tobacco. *Spuntature* were the off cuts of *Sigari Toscani*, the strong black Tuscan cigars. *Spuntature* were a cheap form of pipe tobacco, but certainly not suitable for hand rolled cigarettes.

When Adamo gave me his *cicca* he dared me to take a long drag and inhale deeply. I did just that and the next thing I knew was that I had passed out. Adamo thought it was hilarious but I got really frightened, and after that shock, I was always very careful what kind of *cicca* I accepted.

Mother had not given up her attempts to try and get us repatriated to England. She had been making constant enquiries in Barga and, early summer, she announced that we were going to Florence, to the Offices of the International Red Cross to see whether they could help us.

The journey was quite exciting. We travelled from Barga to Lucca by the *corriera* (postal bus) belonging to a small family firm in Barga called Nardini Bros. The bus was not the most comfortable form of transport. It was an old vehicle with a capacity of about thirty to thirty-five passengers and none too comfortable springing. The roof served as a capacious luggage rack for all manner of goods besides mail.

The travellers were a veritable hotchpotch of humanity. Some people, who like us were going to 'the big city', were dressed in their Sunday best. Others might be peasants who were returning from market laden with packages or even small items of livestock and journeying only part of the way. Each little town had its official stopping place but the bus could be hailed by any intending passenger at any spot en route.

In Lucca mother intended to first go and visit her step aunt, Nella Saporiti, who was really the sister of my grandmother Adele's second husband. On arrival at the Lucca bus terminal, mother hired a horse-drawn carriage to take us to San Donato, the district outside the city walls, where Nella lived.

These open topped horse-drawn carriages are nowadays an expensive tourist attraction but at the time they were an essential taxi service. I remember mother haggling for several minutes with the coachman until he had agreed a price which she thought reasonable.

Nella's house was a fairly big detached villa situated in its own grounds. A reasonably sized garden surrounded the house. It was almost abutting the railway line quite close to a level crossing, and we had great difficulty sleeping at night because of the noise of the trains. Every time a train ran past, the whole house would shake to its very foundations and this kept waking us all up.

Nella lived on the first floor. The ground floor was rented out to a professional couple who had one child, a boy slightly older than myself. This boy unfortunately had some kind of bone disease and could only walk with callipers, and then, only with great difficulty.

We remained here for two nights. San Donato was a fair distance from the actual town. As I could not play with this other boy I spent most of the day watching the relentless march of ants in the garden. At one time I even had the idea of exterminating them but after about fifteen minutes of crushing all the ants in sight, I gave up because more ants kept coming to replace them.

Our journey from Lucca to Florence was by train. Although the third class carriages had hard wooden seats, I wasn't even aware of the discomfort because of the thrill of the journey. In Florence we were going to stay with a lady called Leontina who was a distant cousin of my mother. Florence was like a wonderland after Sommocolonia: so colourful and full of life. From the railway station we caught a tram which took us past the Duomo and the Campanile to the quarter where Leontina lived.

The next morning we went to the offices of the International Red Cross. There they carefully noted down all the particulars of Mother, Aldo and myself. I cannot remember what in fact transpired but Mother said afterwards that the Red Cross official had promised to look into the matter, and although they could not guarantee anything they would certainly be in touch with us in due course.

We took this to mean that, although they were going through the motions, there was very little hope of success and so the next morning we set off again to return to our little mountain village.

At the beginning of that summer a family from Livorno came to stay in Sommocolonia *in villeggiatura* (holiday). They rented an empty house at *Monte*, which in fact belonged to my aunt Argene. The father, who was an engineer, was called Ruggero and his wife was called Wanda. They had two children Nadia, who was about my age and a younger girl called Lauretta.

They had come to spend the months of June, July and August up in the mountains away from the scorching summer heat of the plain. The father travelled back and forth from Livorno, visiting Sommocolonia most weekends. How this family loved staying up in the mountains. To them it was heavenly to be able to get away from the incessant noise and stifling heat of the city. They came back every summer, and continued to do so even after the end of the war. From their very first visit, the house they rented came to be known as Wanda's house.

I took a great fancy to Nadia and I admired her from afar. She had a lithesome figure and she reminded me of a ballerina when she walked. I would have loved to spend a lot of time in the company of Nadia and her family.

Unfortunately, I did not have anything in common with this family, and it would have been rather difficult to justify my presence with them. If Lauretta had been a boy then I might have had an excuse for calling on them.

May and June were wonderful months, for this was the time of year for fireflies. In the early evening, towards dusk, the meadows would be full of thousands of fireflies in flight and their ritual courtship of winking on and off like fairy lights was, and still is, a truly magical sight. I don't think I've ever seen anything to rival this wonderful spectacle of nature. We would have endless fun running around in the meadows, clapping our hands trying to catch the fireflies.

The summers seemed endless to us children. With four months break from school, we had lots of spare time on our hands. During the week we would gather in the *piazza*, those boys who did not have to help their families in the fields, and play cards: *Briscola*, *Scopa* and *Tre Setti* were the three most popular card games.

We would also catch rose chafers; they are really beautiful creatures and their backs are bright green and shiny as if they have been polished. We would tie some cotton thread to one of their legs and in this way make them fly around.

It was great to watch these lovely creatures buzzing around. However I soon became disillusioned because they would frequently break loose and fly off leaving one leg behind in the process. I considered this to be cruel and I therefore stopped catching them. For the same reason I never attempted to catch wall lizards. When caught, they regain their freedom by shedding their tails into your hands.

At other times we might play marbles. Glass marbles were very scarce. The only marbles that were on sale were made of clay. We would normally play a game where the prize was a marble. The winner could have his pick of any of his opponent's marbles.

The clay marbles were rather brittle and they often shattered into little pieces. Consequently the few glass marbles in the village were always highly coveted as prizes. They ended up constantly changing hands.

On Sundays, when everyone was free we would wander around in little gangs looking for mischief. We were always trying to boast of our exploits in front of the girls. One of the most daring and dangerous games we played was destroying wasps' nests. We would set off with bundles of straw looking for these nests.

On finding a wasps' nest, we would proceed to stuff the straw inside and set fire to it. Of course, this made the wasps very angry and they would soon be furiously buzzing around in their hundreds. We would cut off chestnut tree branches and fan the air around us in order to ward off the angry wasps. Invariably we would end up getting stung, sometimes more than once. Some Sundays we might destroy two or even three nests.

One Sunday, after returning to the village from one of our usual 'nest-extermination' raids, we were all boasting, with a great show of bravado, about the number of times we had been stung.

Peppe, Olinto's son, suddenly announced that he had been stung on his scrotum. We all started to laugh and said: "We don't believe you". "But it's true" retorted Peppe. "Show us then", we all began to chant.

At first Peppe refused to even consider it. We kept on ribbing him and calling him a fibber until he eventually yielded. He pulled down his trousers rather reluctantly and sure enough he had three testicles, the third one being a very red and inflamed swelling.

When we saw this we just couldn't contain ourselves with laughter. It must have been very painful for him but he put on a very brave face. Of course Peppe was quite a little hero and after this event, he was known as *"Peppe, tre palle"*.

Those halcyon summer days would be filled with the incessant stridulating noise of the cicadas, which would be replaced, in the evenings, by the chirping sounds of the crickets. At dusk, we would often go round the meadows and stick our fingers in the holes in the grass and pull out the crickets.

On very hot summer evenings, we would sit on the marble steps of the war memorial in front of the church. The marble was nice and cool to sit on. Here we would watch the myriads of stars in the sky and play word games. A very popular one was called 'Guess what Colour'. One of us would say: "I'm thinking of a colour", and the others would take turns at guessing what it was. Of course we would try and think of all kinds of unusual shades of colour. A maximum of five guesses was allowed.

Towards the end of summer, there would be the wheat harvest. Wheat was the second most important crop after chestnuts. The wheat would be harvested by hand but the threshing would be done by machine. A threshing machine could be hired out by the day. It was usually powered by a two-stroke engine. In order to reach the isolated fields, the threshing machine had to be dismantled into manageable, but nevertheless extremely heavy sections.

These bulky sections had to be carried to the appropriate small holding on men's backs. When you consider what heavy weights men had to carry, it was quite incredible that they did not suffer from back troubles.

After the threshing, the sacks of grain would then be taken down to the *mulino*, (water mill), again on men's backs, to be ground into flour. This water mill was the same one, which supplied the village with electricity. The flour was a very important commodity. Not only was it an essential part of the daily diet of the villagers but it also served to pay the miller for his services. It was, of course, whole-wheat flour.

Most of the houses had a specially constructed wood-fired oven. Many families would bake their own bread, usually a week's supply at a time. This whole-wheat bread was much tastier than the rather bland white shop-bought bread on ration.

From time to time we might be lucky enough to be given the odd half loaf (they were usually very large oval shaped loaves weighing well over a kilo each) as a gift. What a delight it was to eat this home made bread together with some cheese and a glass of red wine.

Sometimes, if the bread-making fell on a Sunday or a Holy Day of Obligation, the families would take advantage of this ready heated oven for their roast dinner. After removing the cooked bread from the oven they would insert the joint of meat and potatoes in the oven for cooking.

If ever anything was needed in the way of timber, the men in the village would proceed and make it, whenever possible. The main wood was chestnut in that area and if any beams or planks of wood were required they would seek out a suitable tree, fell it and roughly shape the trunk with axes. Then the trunk would be rolled to a suitable place where it would be marked with string dipped in red dye. Finally two men would proceed to saw it along the previously marked lines with a pit saw.

Chapter 8

Mr Tognarelli, the travel agent was a very strange character indeed, and we boys considered him to be a bit of a freak. He was short and chubby and completely bald. He was also a naturist.

In the summer he would don a kind of jungle suit which consisted of: a short belted tunic, short trousers, a soft round hat with a wide brim all round, knee length stockings and studded mountain boots.

Dressed in this strange garb, he would load his haversack full of stones, and with it slung over his shoulders he would go hiking up into the mountains. When he found a nice quiet little glade he would strip completely and sunbathe in the nude.

Whenever we were alerted that he was heading in the direction of our village we would keep watch to find out where he was going. We would carefully monitor his progress from a safe distance. Then we would go and hide close by and wait for him to settle down in his naturist activity.

When he was blissfully ensconced in his rapport with nature we would suddenly jump out of hiding, shout at the top of our voices and throw stones at him. This would invariably have an electrifying effect on him and to observe him quickly grab his clothes and other belongings and run away stark naked had us all in stitches.

This was the year when I was confirmed. And so I had to attend, along with many other children, catechism classes for about six months. The bishop visited only once every six or seven years and there were consequently quite a lot of candidates for confirmation that year.

One's confirmation day is undoubtedly a memorable event in one's life and everyone in the village ensured that it would be a special feast day. Furthermore, it meant that we would have *un bel pranzo* (a slap up meal) to celebrate this special day. These culinary feasts were all the more enjoyable because they were very rare events.

Late summer was the time of year when itinerant artisans would visit the village. Sometimes they might come every year; if not, every other year. Chief among these was the *stagnino*, literally tinsmith, but he was really the proverbial tinker. He would arrive, after a rather arduous climb up to the village, laden with various pots and pans. He would stay one, two or three days however long it took.

On arrival, he would go round the village ringing a hand bell and shout: "*Stagnino, stagnino*". After ensuring that he had made his presence known to everyone, he would go and install himself in the *piazza* in the shade of one of the two plane trees, ready for business. Although he did have new pots and pans for sale, his main business was mending old pots.

He would carefully cut out any damaged section and apply a new copper patch, which he would rivet to the original pot or receptacle. Then he would carefully beat this patch with a special hammer until he was satisfied with the result. He never hurried his work for he was a real old fashioned artisan. It was fascinating to watch him work. He was always very cheerful: full of spirit, greeting everyone joyfully.

If he was lucky a family would offer him a bed for the night. Otherwise, he would sleep in a hayloft somewhere. He very seldom sold any new pots but this did not dishearten him at all.

Then there was the *arrotino*, (the knife grinder). He would not only sharpen knives but also scissors, scythes and billhooks. The *pennato* or billhook was the main all purpose cutting tool in that region. A man's working clothes were not complete unless he carried a billhook attached to the back of his leather belt. The *arrotino* also sold knives, scissors and other cutting tools.

The *ombrellaio* (the umbrella mender) was also a popular visitor. His main purpose was to mend any broken umbrellas, although he did have new umbrellas for sale. He would recover torn umbrellas and replace any broken spokes. When he had finished his work the umbrella would be as good as new for only a fraction of the cost of a new one.

Last but not least was the *seggiolaio*, (the chair mender). He would set to and re-weave all the worn rush chair seats and replace or mend any sections of the wooden structure that might be broken. Nothing was ever thrown away if there was any chance of mending it.

After having announced their arrival in the village in the same manner as the *stagnino*, all the itinerant artisans would settle down to work in the *piazza*. Apart from villagers bringing them work, they would usually have an audience of appreciative children. They never seemed to mind; in fact they always answered our inquisitive questions with great patience and understanding.

Our neighbour called Giannino, who lived two doors away, was a very strange person. He loved to 'tweak' little boys. He would grab you in the private parts and squeeze very hard. I didn't like this at all and after being caught a couple of times I learnt to keep well clear of him. He was in fact a grandfather and fairly close to seventy years of age. He was always very careful not to do this in the presence of adults.

It was no good complaining because all the men thought that an old man like that was harmless and they regarded his antics as amusing. In the modern world he would most probably have been placed on the paedophile register and might even possibly have been jailed.

There was great excitement in the autumn. One lunchtime, a letter arrived from the International Red Cross. The *postina* (post lady) called Gemma brought the post. Gemma lived in the village. First thing in the morning she would empty the post box in the *piazza* of any outgoing mail and make her way down to the main post office in Barga.

There, she would collect the mail for delivery and then make her way back to Sommocolonia with her satchel full of mail. She would pass by Catagnana (a small village near the bottom of the mountain) and other scattered houses to deliver the mail on her return journey. She would consequently arrive back in Sommocolonia around about midday.

This was a very demanding climb undertaken in all weathers. It was bad enough in the wintertime when the cold and ice could make walking very difficult but I think that it was even worse in the summertime. The heat of the midday day sun was enervating enough without having to struggle up a mountain path with a bagful of mail. And yet, I cannot remember Gemma losing a day's work through illness.

We were all quite tremulous with anticipation when Mother started opening the letter. She read it through and I could see by her expression that the news was not really promising. The International Red Cross had indeed made extensive enquiries for it transpired that they were willing to repatriate me because I was a British citizen, but, as Mother and Aldo were Italian nationals, they could not help them.

If I wished, I could be repatriated via an overland route to North Africa where I would join up with the British authorities there who would make arrangements for me to be taken back home to England.

Inside the envelope was a form, which had to be filled in, and returned to them if I chose to accept their offer. Mother then began to discuss the matter with Grandmother Adele and Dora. They decided that I could have the choice as to whether I wanted to go or not. This was a very weighty decision for a young boy to make. Although I felt good at the fact that I had been given this choice I was really very scared at the thought of the journey on my own.

I then told them that I was declining because I did not want to leave Mother and Aldo on their own. On reflection later, I realised that there was really no choice because I had nowhere to go back to; Father was interned, there was no news of my brother John and we didn't know what conditions were like in England.

In the *piazza* there was a cobbler's shop. The cobbler was called Piero. He was rather an odd character. He was short and chubby and balding considerably. He was a very gentle person and he never hurried. He would often perspire profusely and he was always wiping his brow and baldpate with a large checked handkerchief.

I would frequently wander in and watch Piero at work. I was always a keen observer whenever he was making a pair of new boots. My other main reason for calling there was to see if I could scrounge the odd *cicca* from him. After a while I might say to him: "*Allora Piero, quando la fate una fumata?"* (Well then Piero, when are you going to have a smoke?). If I was lucky he would reply: *"Fra poco"* (Soon). But more often than not he would say: *"Ma l'ho fatta proprio ora."* (I've just had one). After a while I might get sick of hanging around and wander off.

Once a month, Piero would go off to market at Castelnuovo. There he would buy all the goods, which he needed to carry on his trade. He would wander back, late afternoon, usually carrying among other things boot uppers, a roll of leather and one or two old bicycle tyres. He would arrive back in the village puffing and panting after the climb. He was certainly not one of the fittest of men; this was probably inevitable in view of his sedentary occupation.

He was always moaning about the price of leather and other materials and saying that if prices kept going up any further he wouldn't know how he was going to manage.

Most of his work consisted of repairing shoes but he also made shoes and boots to measure. He very seldom made a pair of shoes but he did often make mountain boots for men. If you ordered a pair of boots to be made he would measure your feet in order to purchase the correct size uppers. Then he would place the uppers over a wooden last in the shape of a foot and proceed to build the shoe around it from underneath. Most of the time the boots were all leather with the sole hand sewn to the upper to make it waterproof.

Whenever a potential customer was not happy about the quote, he would tell him that he could save a little money by using a cheaper innersole. Whenever he had to do this he would mumble something to the effect that "spoiling the ship for a 'hap'orth of tar' was really false economy".

The final touches to the boots were when he studded them with hobnails all round, both sole and heel. I used to admire the finished boots and secretly longed to have a pair for myself. This was never to be, for a pair of hand made boots were a luxury that we could not afford. Piero utilised the second hand rubber bicycle tyres for soling and heeling ladies' shoes.

The principal means of transport for goods in the mountains were mules. People normally travelled on foot. If ever any important dignitaries ventured into the village they would usually come up on horseback.

At Ponte di Catagnana, there lived a large extended family nicknamed '*I diavoli*' (the devils). Two of the brothers would frequently pass through Sommocolonia on their way up into the higher mountains with a string of about twelve mules. Several hours later they would return with the mules laden with a cargo of either wood or charcoal. With all the slopes thickly wooded, there was always a plentiful supply of wood for both firewood and charcoal burning. Chestnut wood was also used for the production of tannin.

The '*Diavoli*' family owned a considerable number of large buildings at Ponte di Catagnana, which were used as warehouses. In the busy season these warehouses would be literally crammed full of wood and charcoal. It was always exciting to watch these mules on their way through the village. One could hear the bells attached to the animals from quite a distance and we always tried to guess how many mules there would be in this particular caravan.

One day, we counted over twenty mules but there were four men in charge of them. I always made sure that I stayed well clear of these mules for some of them could be quite vicious and kick violently for no reason at all.

On the slope opposite Sommocolonia on the northern side, about fifteen minutes walk away, there was an isolated cottage where a woman called *La Baregi* lived.

She was married but had no children. Her husband worked in the metallurgical works in Fornaci di Barga. Fornaci di Barga owes the origin of its name to the furnaces in the metal workshops. Fornaci was about ten or eleven kilometres distant, and *La Baregi*'s husband had to travel to and from work on foot. So he usually set off very early in the morning and returned quite late at night. I gathered that his wife was an oversexed buxom woman.

You would quite often hear one of the men in the village say: "I'm feeling a bit randy today. I think I'll pay *La Baregi* a visit ".

Apparently she was quite liberal with her services and would entertain any man free of charge.

She performed a very useful social service. Not only did she keep men happy but I never heard of any women or girls being sexually assaulted or raped in that region. They reckoned that her husband didn't know about her promiscuous activities. It is said that a fool is always happy in his ignorance.

1942 was a very hard year for us. We had no land and therefore had to rely purely on the rations allocated by the Government. There were only about three or four other families in Sommocolonia who, like us, were landless and therefore often had to go hungry.

It was particularly bad for Mother because she would frequently go without any food in order to feed her two children, Aldo and me. The food situation was so bad that you could not even buy any on the black market.

In Italy, it was traditional to make pancakes for the feast of *San Giuseppe*, St Joseph the worker, on the 19th of March. Hearing all the other children looking forward to eating their pancakes not unnaturally made me yearn for some too. We had no fats in the house at the time.

I pleaded so much with my aunt Dora that off she went to try and beg for some form of fat for frying the pancakes. Eventually she was able to find someone who let her have an old rancid scrap of lard. I was told many years later by my aunt that she didn't know how I could have eaten the pancakes but I remember that I enjoyed them very much at the time. There is nothing like adversity to make one appreciate the simple things in life.

Our staple diet consisted mainly of *polenta* made with chestnut flour. It was called *polenta di neccio* or *polenta dolce* (sweet polenta). All the mountains and hills surrounding Sommocolonia were covered in chestnut trees. In fact chestnuts had been providing the main staple diet of the region since time immemorial.

The chestnuts ripened and fell in October. Late October was the time of the chestnut harvest. Every able-bodied man, woman and child would be recruited to help pick up the chestnuts from the ground where they had fallen. It was a backbreaking job bending down all day gathering chestnuts. Also you had to very careful because the outer husks have very sharp painful spines.

Each person was given a kind of pinafore with a very large capacious pocket in front, in which you placed the chestnuts. When the pocket was full you would go along to a central area to empty the chestnuts into sacks. When these sacks were full the strongest men would pick up the full sacks and carry them along to the *metato*, the chestnut-drying shed.

The *metato* was always a small stone built hut with a stone floor. It was invariably built against the mountain so that the opening on the upper floor was at waist height. This opening consisted of a small wooden door, which could be firmly secured. The upper floor was a system of wooden laths, which rested on beams around the walls.

The wooden laths would be set with a very narrow gap between each one. The sacks of fresh chestnuts would be poured onto this wooden floor through the first floor opening. The chestnuts would then be evenly levelled over the floor by means of a very long handled wooden rake.

In order to dry the chestnuts, a fire would be lit in the centre of the stone floor. This fire would be dampened down with the chaff (the dried outer and inner skins of the previous year's harvest). In this manner the chestnuts were dried slowly by the rising hot air. The chestnuts would be turned from time to time to ensure even drying.

The whole process of drying would take about three to four weeks. It could not be hurried. In fact I learnt that many years previous, one of the families thought they would be clever and hasten the drying process by using a roaring open wood fire. The result was that the *metato* caught fire and burnt down.

When the drying process was completed the chestnuts had to be threshed. A small communally owned chestnut threshing machine, powered by a two stroke engine, would be dismantled into manageable sections and transported on men's backs to each *metato* in turn. The threshing machine would then be reassembled and the work of separating the skins from the dried nuts would begin.

The shelled chestnuts would be filled into sacks and the dry chaff (*pula*) would be stored for use the following year. The dried chestnuts would then be taken down to the *mulino* (water mill) at the *corsonna* river to be ground into flour.

This *mulino* was also the source of electricity for the village. The water mill drove a dynamo, which produced a small amount of electricity. The electricity was 100/150 volts. The supply to the village was carried by means of two single strands of wire supported by wooden poles driven into the ground at about twenty-five yard intervals.

This private electricity supply was anything but reliable. There were frequent disruptions to the supply for a variety of reasons and I reckon that in the worst months of the winter the supply was off more often than it was on. Each house was only allowed to run two light bulbs, about 50 watts maximum. Consequently everyone relied on inefficient carboy or oil lamps. The only electrical appliances in the village were the two small radio sets belonging to the priest and the *Dopolavoro*.

About once a year, when the owner of the mill came up to the village to collect the paltry sum of approximately twenty pence from each household for the year's supply of electricity he was always greeted with moans. He would be chastised not only for the frequent loss of power but also for the 'extortionate' cost of the electricity.

A sufficient number of sacks of chestnut flour would be retained for personal consumption throughout the year. It would be stored in large wooden chests (made of chestnut wood of course) in the basement. The remaining chestnut flour was then treated as a cash crop and would be sold on the open market. It was undoubtedly a very useful source of income for those families who had large tracts of chestnut woods.

Chestnut *polenta* formed a major part of the villagers' diet at that time. It would be eaten at least once and sometimes twice a day in the winter. It would also be eaten very frequently in the summer. It would normally be eaten hot with *biroldo*, (black pudding) or local cheese, either cow's or sheep's (*pecorino*).

On a cold winter's day hot *polenta* with black pudding could be quite nice. But, chestnut *polenta* is extremely rich and not to be recommended for a year round staple diet for growing children. Eating *polenta* day in and day out I developed worms, which gave me terrible anal pruritus.

An interesting point about chestnuts is their nutritional value. As opposed to other nuts they have a high water content and very little oil, making them virtually fat free.   They are high in carbohydrates, contain high quality protein, and are gluten and cholesterol free. This may be one of the main reasons for the longevity of many people in that region. Prior to the introduction of maize from the New World, *polenta* in Europe was always made with chestnut flour.

Chestnut flour was also used to make *castagnaccio* a local cake flavoured with pine nuts, olive oil and rosemary. It was quite nice because it was only eaten occasionally and then just in small quantities.

Another tasty dish made with chestnut flour was *necci*. These were chestnut flour pancakes. They were cooked on special iron plates over the large wooden fire in the kitchen.

In the spring, the shepherds from the mountains above Sommocolonia would walk down through the village on their way to market at Barga with basketfuls of fresh ricotta. The ricotta would be wrapped in chestnut leaves. We would from time to time treat ourselves to a ricotta or two. Hot *necci* filled with freshly made ricotta were a real treat.

I always looked forward to chestnut harvest time because whenever you were asked to help with the harvest you were assured of being well fed. At lunchtime, of course, it would be *polenta* with *biroldo* or cheese, but in the evening you would go back to their house for the main meal of the day. This was very often *tagliarini*, which I always looked forward to eating.

Tagliarini is a local dish consisting of fresh homemade 'tagliatelle-shaped' pasta strips cooked in a soup of borlotti beans and diced potatoes. *Tagliarini* eaten with home made wholemeal bread is a delight, which I relish to this day: truly one of the great peasant dishes of the region.

At chestnut harvest time we would often eat *ballucci*, boiled chestnuts, in the evenings. Families who owned chestnut woods would set aside one or more sacks full of selected chestnuts. These would be used for *mondine* (roast chestnuts), in the winter.

On long winter nights it was the custom to go to *veglia*, to spend the evening in a neighbour's house chatting about various matters. If we were lucky the host family might decide to have a roast chestnut evening. So a large capacious pan shaped rather like a frying pan with holes in the base would be filled with chestnuts. This pan had a long wooden handle and it would be placed over a roaring wood fire.

The pan was made of quite heavy metal and when it was filled with chestnuts it was very heavy indeed. One of the men would be in charge of turning the chestnuts from time to time so as to prevent them being burnt. This would be done by continually tossing them, a rather strenuous exercise.

When the roast chestnuts were ready the pan would be removed from the fire and placed on the stone floor in the middle of the room. Then everyone was invited to help him or herself. The roast chestnuts would be washed down with *vinella*, local wine with a rather low alcohol content. The children were also allowed to have some *vinella* suitably watered down.

Frequently, someone would read stories out loud from a book, because many of the older people could not read. I remember being asked on several occasions to read a book for the benefit of everyone gathered around the roaring fire. It seemed that I had a good reading voice at the time. Also by the very dim light of an oil lamp one needed the keen eyesight of youth to be able to clearly see the small print in the book.

At other times people would just tell stories: fairy tales or ghost stories. The ghost stories were really the most popular. For some strange reason human beings seem to revel in being thoroughly scared by ghoulish tales. Two particular tales that I remember were the following.

The first was a story about a young bride who had been murdered one night on the road leading to her home. This had taken place at a village quite some distance away from our area. On moonlit evenings she would frequently appear to people walking by and she would ask them to pray for her soul. Many were frightened to go out at night for fear of meeting her.

Then one day, one of the villagers said that he was going to put paid to this story once and for all. That evening he set off with a loaded shotgun to look for the ghost. As he rounded a bend in the narrow road he was suddenly confronted by the phantasmal figure. He then raised his shotgun and fired at the ghost, which seemed to fall and then disappear: "There, that's the last we'll see of her" he muttered to himself and turned round to go back home.

He had only gone a few yards when the ghost suddenly reappeared in front of him and held out a hand to him saying: "There's your bullet back." At this the man dropped down dead of sheer fright.

The second story concerns an incident, which happened to one of the inhabitants of Sommocolonia many years before the war. The *camposanto*, (cemetery) of the village, is situated about a kilometre from the village itself. The track that led from the village to *campeglio* and *Montebono* skirted the upper wall of the *camposanto*. From here one had a very clear view looking down on the whole of the cemetery.

One winter's evening, a man from the village was returning home alone, at round about midnight, after spending all day hunting game. As he was passing the cemetery he saw the most peculiar sight he had ever seen. There in the middle of the cemetery was this big pink elephant and dancing all around it were these little pink baby elephants. The man took one look, dropped his shotgun in fright and ran home as fast as his legs could carry him.

The next morning, he was recounting this experience to a couple of his friends. The latter decided to go along and investigate the matter. When they reached the cemetery they were able to explain the strange phenomenon of the previous night. Apparently a bitch had given birth to a litter of puppies and what he had really seen was the mother dog and the little baby pups shuffling around it.

The whole scene had been lit up in a pinkish glow by the action of 'ignis fatuus', the will of the wisp, which is caused by the gases rising from the graves and spontaneously igniting. Although the man had seen a dog and its puppies, because of the strange circumstances, the phenomenon had been magnified in his mind to represent a large elephant surrounded by baby elephants.

There were two families who regularly invited us to help them with the chestnut harvest. The first was my aunt Argene, my father's sister. Argene was a very quiet and gentle lady and she was always very kind to me. Although she would be dressed in black she was definitely a notch above the peasant women of the village. She had two daughters, Gina and Maria, who were several years older than me.

I'll always remember gathering chestnuts at *La Madonnina* with my two cousins because it was on a very exposed windy slope, north of the village. The song *vento*, which has now been recorded by Pavarotti and many other singers, had just been released then and was all the rage. We would sing at the top of our voices: "*Vento, vento, portami via con te*" and so forth whilst we gathered chestnuts.

The second family was the Passerotti family. Their woodlands were at *Pruno* which was on the way down to Barga and was situated in a more sheltered area. They also had a few fields here and they had built a small stone house, consisting of one large room with a stable attached to it. In one corner of the room there were a couple of bunk beds.

At grain harvest time and other busy periods, one or two members of the family could sleep on these bunks. In this way they didn't have to waste any valuable hours going back to the village about two to two-and-a-half kilometres away: they could literally work from dawn to dusk.

Another occasion when we might have a great feed was for the *cena del cicio* (the pig's supper). *Cicio* is a dialectal word for *maiale*. The term 'the pig's supper' was really a misnomer because the poor pig wasn't invited to the meal; rather he provided the meal.

Several families in Sommocolonia would rear a pig to be eventually killed for food. In October they would go off to market at *Castelnuovo* and come back with a little piglet on their shoulders. After fattening this pig all year long, they would slaughter it the following September.

I particularly remember the pig that was slaughtered by my paternal grandmother, *Nonna* Maria, my aunt Rosina and her family. I was never really very close to *Nonna* Maria or Aunt Rosina. The two ladies were always dressed in black. Aunt Rosina had started to lose several teeth. *Nonna* Maria only had a couple of blackened front teeth left so that, when she smiled, it could be quite frightening to a young child.

Uncle Fiore was a taciturn person and everybody considered him to be rather strange. He was very much a solitary type and, from time to time, he would go off, all on his own, into the higher mountains for several days on end.

I gather that, whenever there was a difference of opinion, *Nonna* Maria would repeatedly remind him that he was living in **her** house. Aunt Rosina would invariably side with *Nonna* Maria. And so, Fiore's strangeness was most probably due to the fact that he felt downtrodden by the two overbearing ladies in his family.

Fiore would also alternate between periods of lethargy and frenetic activity. Whenever he managed to galvanise himself into action he worked at a feverish pace. If he was pruning trees he would clamber up and down the tree trunks like a monkey and work at twice the rate of a normal man.

There was a chap in the village who was the official pig killer and he would go round all the families in turn. First of all he stunned the pig with a special gun, then stretched the animal out on a wooden ladder and quickly proceeded to stick a knife in its jugular vein to drain off all the blood. After that he shaved off all the hard bristles on the skin with hot water and a cutthroat razor.

Then along with uncle Fiore he carried the ladder with the pig into the cellar. Here the pig was hoisted up by its rear legs and tied to one of the beams. After hanging up the animal in this manner, the pig slaughterer would slit open the front of the carcase from top to bottom and remove all the intestines and innards. The intestines and the bladder were then collected into pails.

After that the pig slaughterer took the intestines down to *Rio* the nearest river, where he very thoroughly washed them clean. Further down the stream there might be a housewife who was rinsing her washing but this was of no import to the pig slaughterer. He then brought back the skins to be used for making the sausages and the *biroldo*.

On returning to the village this master butcher quartered the animal and cut up the various sections ready for seasoning. The legs were kept and seasoned for *prosciutto* or raw hams. In the evening there was a big meal when all the sections of the pig that could not easily be preserved were cooked and served up as a glorious feast to which many relations were invited.

The *cena del cicio* was indeed a gargantuan repast to be remembered. Of course if you reared a pig you had to declare it to the authorities and your meat ration would be proportionately reduced.

Years later when I thought back on this ritual of slitting open the pig I would cringe at the thought of the barbaric custom in the Middle Ages when human beings were often hung drawn and quartered in a similar manner, whilst still alive.

Chapter 9

1942 was not a year that I look back on with any great nostalgia, for it was really the only time during my five and a half year 'holiday' that I fell ill.

It happened sometime in May when I was out playing in the woods with a friend. Suddenly, without any prior warning, I started having a very queasy stomach. When I stopped to spend a penny I noticed that my urine was very dark brown, so dark in fact that it was staining the stones on the path. I slowly made my way home and I was feeling so ill that I couldn't remember the journey back.

When I told Mother how ill I was feeling, she put me straight to bed and went down to the public telephone in the village shop to ring Dr Serafini, the *medico condotto*, the family doctor assigned to the village. In reply the doctor told Mother to ensure that I stayed in bed well wrapped, with no food.

The following day, my skin went all yellow and there were white patches in my stools. Mother went back to telephone the doctor, who on being described these symptoms, diagnosed that I had a severe dose of *itterizie*, yellow jaundice. The treatment was for me to stay in bed and starve it out. I had to have nothing to eat or drink except sips of plain water.

I felt extremely ill and I ended up remaining in bed for at least ten days without food or drink. There was an epidemic of yellow jaundice that year and a lot of the children in the village had caught it. The other children were not showing the severe symptoms that I had. Whereas my skin had gone quite yellow all over, they had merely developed a yellow colouring round the pupils of their eyes.

I am sure that everyone thought I was going to die because no one ever came to see me while I was bedridden. Although all the other children got over their jaundice within a matter of a week or two it took the best part of six months for me to fully recover from it.

I was so ill that Mother would have done anything to make me better. A remedy recommended by some of the older women in the village was that I should swallow fifteen live head lice. These apparently would devour the disease and make me better. I was almost on the point of following this old wives' remedy. The only thing that prevented me doing so was the fact that you had to first find the lice and then catch them.

When the doctor eventually decided that I could at last get up out of bed, I found that I was very weak and could barely walk downstairs. It was now time to start eating again. On the first day, I was allowed one small *zucchino* (baby marrow) which had to be boiled in plain water without any seasoning. The only flavouring I was allowed was a little olive oil poured over it. I did not really like *zucchini* but that particular one was very enjoyable.

And so little by little I started eating a bit more each day, all plainly cooked and it was not until three months later that the doctor finally declared me cured. However, as I have already mentioned, I did not feel my old self again until after about six months' convalescence.

Whilst I was lying in bed with yellow jaundice, I kept thinking about my childhood in England for I had been a very sickly child and had caught every children's disease that was going. I particularly remember being very ill with scarlet fever. In fact, the doctor had not given much hope of my survival.

Then, suddenly, one day I began to feel better and the doctor declared that I was now over the worst of the disease and on the way to recovery. Mother had bought me lots of toys, jigsaws and comics to keep me amused. I was very sad when we had to dispose of all these items because the disease was very contagious.

Many was the time that I would be lying in bed in the room above the shop premises listening to the advertising sign swaying in the wind. This was the very room where I was born. On the wall outside the shop there was a metal advertising sign for Players cigarettes with the famous slogan 'Players Please'. The hinges of this sign were rather rusty and it would squeak incessantly as it swung back and forth in the wind.

Sweets and chocolates were not officially rationed in Italy during the war. They were in effect rationed by price, for they were very expensive. In fact the village shop did not sell any sweets. In Barga you could buy chocolates in one or two of the cafés. Actual boxes of chocolates were a rarity indeed in that region.

There would usually be a jar of chocolates standing on the counter of these cafés in Barga. Each chocolate would be wrapped in silver paper and they were sold individually. During the whole of my stay in Sommocolonia during the war I was lucky enough to have a single chocolate on only a very few special occasions.

During my convalescence my mother would, every now and then, bring me back from Barga one sugared almond as a special treat. This was to cheer me up for I was quite depressed due to my illness. Sugared almonds were a lot cheaper than chocolates. What a contrast to what I had been used to in my childhood in England!

In June, Signora Casciani retired. I was due to finish my primary schooling at the end of that month. All the other children of my age in the village would then be free to go and help their families with the daily drudgery of rural life in the fields. Signora Casciani had told my mother that I was quite an intelligent boy and that I should really continue my studies and attend the *Scuola Media* (Middle school for children aged eleven to fourteen) in Barga.

Fortunately for me Mother had been convinced and so I was due to start a new school in the autumn. I was a little apprehensive at the thought, because I would be the only child from the village going down to Barga to school every day.

There were, and still are, two churches in Sommocolonia. The main church is called the church of *San Frediano* (Saint Frigidian). Saint Frigidian is reputed to have been an Irish abbot-bishop of the sixth century. The second church is a small chapel in the *piazza* called *San Rocco* (St Rock). St Rock was a fourteenth century French Saint who, whilst travelling through Italy on his way to Rome, had saved the local populace from the Plague. St Rock is always portrayed showing the characteristic black ulcer of the plague on his upper leg.

One day in late summer, I was playing with some other boys near the main church. We were amusing ourselves throwing stones at each other. Someone threw a large stone, which landed on the square in front of the church.

At that moment the priest, Don Fredianelli, came out to see what all the commotion was about. Everyone had disappeared except me. The priest called me over and asked me about the stone. I told him that it was not me who had thrown it. He nevertheless told me to pick it up. Whilst I was doing this he gave me a *nocchino* on my head. He had a very huge embossed ring of the type that were used as seals in olden times.

He hit me very hard on the head with this ring. This really hurt me very much; in fact I saw stars. I immediately dropped the stone, turned round to the priest and called him a *Maledetto Rospo* (an Accursed Toad). I then ran away home to the other end of the village.

The priest was flat-footed and I could hear him running after me with the 'cha, cha' sound of his footsteps. Fortunately he was unable to catch me because he was rather hindered by the full-length soutane which he always wore.

Nevertheless he followed me all the way home where I quickly told Mother what had happened and dashed upstairs into the bedroom. I could hear the priest arguing with Mother downstairs. I thought I was going to be in terrible trouble but it transpired that Mother believed my account of events. In fact she chastised the priest for hitting me so hard with his ring.

In the autumn, we went to help Aunt Rosina and family with the grape harvest at *Colto*. Everyone old enough had to help and each one of us was given a pair of scissors to cut the bunches of grapes from the vines, and a bucket to place them in. When the buckets were full we would shout and Uncle Fiore would come and collect them and empty them into a large open-topped wooden vat in the cellar of the day hut they had built on the smallholding.

The grapes were of mixed varieties and it was quite exciting to try them all. Some tasted awful but there were others, which were quite nice. Whenever I found a variety which I liked I would proceed to have my fill. My cousin Renzo was a bit of a *matterello*, daft, and he was always threatening to do crazy things.

One day, after lunch he was in the row of vines next to me when he casually announced "I think I'll cut my tongue". At that, he placed the scissors to his mouth and he in fact did accidentally cut his tongue. His tongue then started bleeding profusely; I have never seen anything bleed so heavily. He began to cry and shout that he was going to die. His mother Rosina started yelling and it was all a pandemonium. There was no more harvesting done that day. Renzo on the other hand had learnt a salutary lesson, for he was a lot quieter and less foolish after that.

In mid-September the new schoolmistress arrived. She was called Signora Cassettari. She was a widow and had two children: a girl called Dora who was four years older than me, and a boy named Orlando, who was my age. They rented the flat on the top floor of Olinto's house.

I was very lucky indeed for this meant that I would have a companion who would be attending middle school with me. At the beginning of October, Orlando and I started at the *Scuola Media* in Barga. This meant getting up earlier than usual for we had a five-kilometre walk to school every morning.

Going down to Barga was quite easy, for we would run down the mule path. We would invariably take the *scorciatoia* (short cut) which went straight down through Catagnana and rejoined the *mulattiera* (mule track) just before *Ponte di Catagnana*. About two hundred yards further down was the main road. From here it was just over a kilometre's walk to Barga on the *Strada Maestra* (the main road).

The journey back home was a lot more strenuous as we had a long climb back up to Sommocolonia. It would have been a very monotonous drag had I been on my own. With Orlando to keep me company the return journey was not so bad for we would slowly wend our way up the *mulattiera* chatting and joking and the time would pass quickly. The most difficult section was the last part, which was quite steep, especially in the heat of the summer.

About four fifths of the way up the mountain track there was a small chapel called *San Rocchino* (little St Rock). The door of this chapel consisted of a metal grid and it was always kept locked. I cannot remember any church functions ever taking place in this chapel.

For some reason people would toss the occasional coin through the metal grid and on the floor of the chapel there was always a fair smattering of coins.

At the front of the chapel there was a little portico with a low wall on one side. This wall was just the right height for sitting on. As the chapel was surrounded by full-grown chestnut trees, it provided an ideal shaded resting place.

We would often rest here on our way back home. I would sit there eyeing all the coins and imagining what I could do with that money. To me it seemed like a lot of money but it probably only amounted to a few lire.

In our present day selfish secular society this chapel would have presented a 'heaven-sent' opportunity for opportunists to break in. At that time I never heard of any occasion when this chapel had been broken into. To steal that money would most probably have been considered the equivalent of committing a cardinal sin.

One morning in January 1943, we awoke to find it had snowed quite heavily during the night. The snow was lying a good ten to twelve inches deep. I went up to seek Orlando as usual and found that he was moaning and groaning, saying that he definitely did not want to go to school because of the weather.

When Orlando saw me he eventually agreed to go to school. I remember his mother saying to him: "Orlando, you had better have some raw eggs to keep the cold out". So she mixed a couple of raw eggs in milk and *marsala* which he proceeded to swallow.

I was very envious because all I had consumed for breakfast was a hard crust of bread with a glass of very milky coffee. It was a very raw morning and how I wished that I could have had some raw eggs to keep out the cold! Also, Orlando was wearing a brand-new pair of *scarponi* (studded boots), something I had always longed to have.

We set off at our usual pace running down the *mulattiera*. Orlando was in front of me and we had gone about half a kilometre when he suddenly skidded and disappeared completely under the snow. I stood there utterly flabbergasted and hesitated for a few moments.

Then I proceeded to dig him out and started to rub him all over because he was shivering quite violently. After about five minutes he began to recover and eventually we set off again on our journey to school. My thoughts at the time were: "*Povero Orlando, non ti hanno salvato nemmeno le uova*" (Poor Orlando, even the raw eggs couldn't save you from the cold).

Orlando was not very highly motivated in respect of schoolwork. His mother wanted to help by giving him extra tuition at home. However he would not hear of it unless his school mate Bernard was allowed to come along. I was very grateful for this because here I was having extra private tuition at no cost.

A lot of the work was centred on the Italian language and grammar. Signora Cassettari would ask questions such as: "What is the third person singular of the pluperfect subjunctive of the verb *salire* (to ascend)?" Orlando was still not very keen and it was invariably me who came out with the correct answer.

On the other hand, I used to love this sense of competition and in this way I became very proficient in Italian grammar and could conjugate even the most difficult verbs just as easily as reciting 'times tables' in maths.

Chapter 10

Life in the village was totally centred on the church. Sundays and Holy Days of Obligation were the only times when most people had a really good meal.

Easter was a special time because not only was it the biggest feast day in the Catholic calendar but in Sommocolonia it also happened to be the *quarant'ore*. The *quarant'ore* was (and still is to a lesser extent) a period of forty hours of special devotions. The time of the year for the forty hours devotions varied from parish to parish.

At Easter, the church in Sommocolonia would be specially decorated and the altar would be built up with extra sections to accommodate well over one hundred candles. When all these extra candles were lit for the special Easter church functions, the main altar would shine radiantly bright.

During the three days of Easter (Sunday, Monday and Tuesday), there would be extra masses and vespers each day. About four priests including the provost from Barga would come and stay in the presbytery.

One of the priests would say mass and the other clergy would assist acting as deacons and sub-deacons. At this stage the ancient practice of concelebrating mass had not yet been reintroduced into the life of the church. It was only re-established as a result of Vatican II (*Sacro Sanctum Concilium* 1963).

I liked attending all the major church functions. I particularly enjoyed participating in sung vespers on Sunday afternoons. I had always wanted to be an altar boy but I never got the opportunity. There were already far too many boys on the altar. Besides I was far too timid to put forward my views or promote my wishes.

Easter Tuesday was the day when friends and relatives from Barga and all the surrounding villages would come to visit. With the influx of visitors the number of people in the village would swell to more than double on that day.

The villagers would cook special cakes to regale their guests. Among these were *Torta di farro* (spelt cake), *Torta di Riso* (rice cake) and *Torta di Mandorle* (almond cake). The *Torta di Farro* was a type of savoury flan and I did not like it at all. The other two were sweet open topped tarts. They were usually flavoured with *Sassolino*, a liqueur, and I thought they were delicious. I used to love all these *feste* and I always looked forward to Easter time.

For the three days of the Easter festival a couple of market stalls would be set up in the *piazza* and traders from Barga would sell various kinds of goodies and cheap novelties. The stalls would be laden with such things as novelty hats, home cooked biscuits, crunchy nut toffee and myriads of other inexpensive items. And so the village square would take on a festive atmosphere, which together with all the extra visitors, made it a very exciting time for children.

Early on Easter Sunday morning in 1943, Grandmother Adele died. She had been ill for some time. About ten days before Easter she went into a coma. The doctor was unable to make a proper diagnosis. Mother and Aunt Dora decided to request a visit from a *professore*, (a specialist) from Pisa. He came up to Sommocolonia on horseback on Maundy Thursday.

The *professore* was a very imposing looking gentleman. His whole deportment certainly commanded respect. After examining Grandmother Adele, he mentioned something about her kidneys and declared: *"Purtropp non c'è niente da fare. E' solo questione di tempo."* (I'm afraid there is nothing I can do. It's only a matter of time), intimating days rather than weeks.

After the visit he asked if he could wash his hands. Toilet soap was unobtainable in the shops, so the specialist was handed a new bar of cheap household carbolic soap and a brand new towel. I was absolutely astonished at the manner in which he washed his hands. He washed and rubbed his hands over and over again for several minutes and when he had finished, they could have been clean enough to perform an operation. I do not know what it cost to call out a specialist all the way from Pisa but I should think that the expense must have been quite considerable.

The only other time I remember a *professore* being summoned to Sommocolonia was to examine a village lady called Mrs Guidi. This *professore* also came up to the village on horseback for the trek up the mountain on foot was not for the likes of such professional men.

His diagnosis on Mrs Guidi was that she had double pneumonia. In those days before the development of antibiotics there was really no effective treatment for pneumonia. The specialist declared that the disease would just have to take its course. I remember thinking at the time: "**Double** pneumonia. She must be very seriously ill indeed!" Despite this Mrs Guidi not only recovered but she lived until well into her eighties.

Losing Grandmother Adele was a sad event for all of us for she was such a lovable person. What made it even worse for me was that, out of respect for poor Grandmother Adele, I was forbidden to go out and play with other children. And this at the most exciting time of the year in Sommocolonia.

As soon as Grandmother Adele died, a carpenter in the village, set to, making her coffin. This was the normal thing for there were no ready-made coffins in those days. The coffin was completed within hours. Then Grandmother Adele was laid out in her coffin in the sitting room for the next two days. Four large candlesticks were placed at the four corners of the coffin, and many villagers called in to pay their last respects. Several women took turns to say prayers and keep vigil over her body day and night.

The funeral took place on Easter Tuesday and because of the special feast day the village was full of visitors. Consequently at least three hundred people, an enormous crowd for an ordinary village funeral, must have accompanied the coffin to the cemetery.

Eight pallbearers of the village *Misericordia* took turns to carry Grandmother Adele to the *camposanto*. The *Misericordia* was originally a confraternity that had been established by the church sometime in the Middle Ages. Its members consisted of able-bodied men of the community and its functions were to perform special duties for the sick and the dead. They would carry ill patients to hospital when necessary and the deceased to the cemetery. Even to this day many of the ambulance services in the smaller towns in Italy are still called *Misericordia* and are often manned by unpaid volunteers.

Grandmother Adele's body was laid to rest in a *forno*. *Forno* in this context means burial niche. These *forni* are still a popular form of burial in present day Italy. The are in fact burial chambers somewhat reminiscent of the burial chambers in the catacombs of the early church.

However, unlike those early *in loco* burial chambers of the catacombs, the modern *forni* are purpose built and above ground. The coffins are slotted into the wall, head first, so to speak, and the small external opening is then sealed by being cemented. The sealed square is later finished by being faced with a marble plaque. This plaque is normally inscribed with an appropriate epitaph and a photo of the deceased. The spaces in these *forni* have to be purchased from the local authority but they do ensure that the bodies will not be disturbed by subsequent burials.

Easter time was also very welcome because it represented the start of spring and the reawakening of nature for another year. Thus people would celebrate by wearing new clothes for the first time.

There was not really any system whereby the public could buy fireworks in Italy. Only local authorities organised special fireworks displays. Wartime had put a stop to these, at least in the Barga region. It was the custom however that people would let off *petardi* on Holy Saturday. *Petardi* were small 'bangers' and these would be bought at Easter time. In Sommocolonia where money was short, the boys had developed their own system for letting off *petardi*.

Gunpowder was not generally on sale but it could be made. Potassium nitrate (saltpetre) tablets were sold by chemists as a medicament for sore throats, and these tablets could be bought at will by adults.

Although we children were not allowed to purchase potassium nitrate tablets, we could always find some adult who would buy them on our behalf. These tablets of potassium nitrate would be ground into powder. Then the ground powder would be mixed with sulphur and ground charcoal. The eventual amalgamation of these various powders resulted in a crude form of gunpowder.

It was usual to place a single tablet dose on a flat stone and stand firmly with the heel of one shoe on this mixture. By sharply clicking the free heel against the other one you could produce quite a loud bang.

One day, Benito wanted to show off in front of the girls and he thought that he would try a three-tablet mixture. It certainly made a much louder bang but the heel of his shoe went flying off at the speed of a rocket. Fortunately, nobody was injured and we confined ourselves to the usual dosage after that.

Still, boys will be boys. We hatched a plot to let off a really big one – twenty tablets! We went up into the high ground at the northern edge of the village. There we found a flat spot with a protruding stretch of land above it, behind which we could safely hide. We looked for a suitably wide flat stone. We carefully positioned this stone, then we ground up all the mixture and placed the powder in a pile on the stone. On top of this we placed another flat stone. Finally we stood on the overhang ready to drop another heavy stone on to it.

When we let this stone drop there was an almighty explosion as of a bomb being dropped. The noise reverberated all round the valleys and the stones shattered into a small avalanche down the mountainside. We got really frightened and never tried anything so daring again.

1943 was very special because it was the year that I made my first communion. The first communion was always made on the feast of Corpus Domini (nowadays called Corpus Christi) in June. It was one of the most memorable highlights of my childhood. That year there were eleven candidates for first communion, the largest number for a long time.

To mark this special day I had brand new clothes to wear: a navy blue suit, a white shirt, black shoes, and white gloves. I was also given a new prayer book and a rosary. Then I had a formal photograph taken on the terrace above the *canonica*.

The best was yet to come. After the ceremony we celebrated with a very special meal: *maccheroni* as a first course, followed by roast meat and trimmings for main course and fruit for dessert. *Maccheroni* are a dish of homemade pasta torn into rough shapes. After cooking, the pasta shapes are layered along with Bolognese sauce into a large serving bowl. With a generous sprinkling of grated cheese they are one the world's most delightful dishes. The cheese of course was *pecorino (sheep's cheese)* because at that time *parmigiano* was unobtainable.

To top it all, Mother had bought me four sugared almonds wrapped in a cellophane packet. Four sugared almonds! This was luxury indeed!

Even the church bells acclaimed the merits of home made *maccheroni* in the following ditty, which the children used to chant:

> Din, dan, don
> Le campan di Castiglion
> Una cuce, una taglia,
> una fa il cappel di paglia.
> Una fa i maccheroni,
> incaciati belli e buoni.
>
> Din, dan don
> Say the bells of Castiglion.
> One's busy cutting, another sewing,
> A third is making a straw hat.
> Another is making maccheroni
> With lots of cheese for all to please.

I felt very special on the day of my first communion and as I strutted 'vainly,' around the village, I thought I was a little angel. I behaved 'impeccably' and didn't harbour an impure thought all day.

The next big event in the church calendar was the feast of the *Madonna del Carmine*, our Lady of Mount Carmel, on the sixteenth of July.

This feast was (and still is) celebrated triennially in Sommocolonia with a special procession. The processional route would be especially adorned for this religious feast day. Archways, interwoven with box, would be erected at various points around the village. Householders would hang suitable drapes outside their windows.

The children were entrusted with the task of going round all the dwellings in the neighbouring hamlets and *palazzi*, asking for flowers with which to decorate the village. The petals would then be strewn all over the village streets.

Towards evening there would be a special service in honour of Our Lady. This would culminate in the statue of Our Lady being carried in procession through the village over a carpet of flowers. All the villagers would participate in this torchlight procession, reciting the rosary and singing appropriate hymns in honour of Our Lady. Practically everyone would take part, even those few people who hardly ever attended church throughout the year.

The *Comune* had decided that year that all the houses in Sommocolonia should be properly numbered. And so, in the summer a small band of Council workmen came up to the village to carry out this task. They cemented small marble plaques with the appropriate number and the name of the street on each house. Large name plaques were also affixed to the houses at both ends of each street. Many people found out that the street they were living in had been known by a different name from the one allocated by the Council; quite amusing really.

The *Scuola Media* had a scheme whereby pupils would be given work to do during the long summer holidays. And so Orlando and I were given a folder entitled *Compiti per le vacanze*, homework for the holidays. This consisted of a series of exercises to be performed on a weekly basis. The two main subjects covered were Italian and Maths.

Just around the corner from the *piazza* lived a chap called Pietrino Moscardini. He was in fact Benito's uncle. This Pietrino had been given the nickname *Il Monchetto* (maimed person).

He had been in a shooting accident several years earlier whilst out hunting with his brother Cecco (Benito's father). His gun went off accidentally and he consequently lost an arm. As he was a *mutilato*, (disabled person) he was appointed a part time civil servant. His duties were to deliver to the village all official documents relating to land tax, housing, water and other local government matters.

During the war, these duties also included delivering ration books to every family. The ration books were issued each month. Pietrino was one of the few adults in the village who were literate and he would willingly help anyone who had any difficulty in filling out official forms. It was amazing to see how he managed to skilfully write and fill out forms with only one arm.

Netto, the shop proprietor, had decided that the time had come for him to retire. His son Piero did not want to follow his father in the business and so the shop licences were being surrendered.

A fellow called Vittorio Vincenti applied for the transfer of the licences to his name and as he was the only person interested he was immediately successful. Vittorio was also the *Consigliere* (official representative) of the village. The village shop provided a very essential service to the village and it was paramount that someone competent should carry it on. And so the shop was transferred to Vittorio's house at *Monticino,* which happened to be quite close to our house.

Apart from an area for the sale of essential foodstuffs, Vittorio's shop also had a room large enough to be converted into a small meeting place. Three round tables were installed and the men could go there to play cards and have a drink. It provided a more comprehensive service than the *Dopolavoro,* because for the first time here was a rendezvous, which could be frequented by women and children.

Vittorio was also a very active member of the Fascist Party. As such he was entrusted with the supervision of the *Rocca.* The *Rocca,* meaning fortress, was in fact the surviving section of the inner fortified keep of the medieval defences of the village.

This comprised a stretch of land and a tower. The tower was the only remaining one of two that had been erected in the Middle Ages. It was built of stone and very impregnable. It had three storeys and each storey had a wooden floor. All around, there were narrow embrasures for the firing of arrows and small arms.

The top storey was battlemented with a stone floor. This latter was to render it fireproof. At the base, the walls were over two metres thick and even at the top they were well over a metre wide. The tower held a dominant position in the village.

From the top of the tower you had an unobstructed view of the whole surrounding area. Whenever official visitors came to Sommocolonia they invariably wished to see the view from the top of the tower. Vittorio Vincenti, the guardian would take them on a guided tour.

I remember one day when some important looking people arrived in the village. They wanted to know if it was possible to climb to the top of the ancient tower. I took them along to see Vittorio. I casually asked if I could come along as well. To my astonishment, Vittorio replied: "*Ma certo*" (of course you can). When I reached the top of the tower I was absolutely astounded at the incredible commanding view of the surrounding valleys and mountains.

Bernard Moscardini's First Communion photograph in 1943. Taken on the terrace of the 'canonica'.

The village cemetery. The 'forni' burial chambers can clearly be seen.

The 'devil's bridge' at Borgo a Mozzano.

The small chapel of 'San Rocchino'. Note the 'mulattiera' (mule track).

Chapter 11

Sommocolonia is situated on a hilltop approximately seven hundred and ten metres above sea level. Its name originates from the Latin '*summa colonia*' meaning settlement on the summit.

The Romans had established a fortified outpost on this hilltop because of its commanding position over the *Serchio* valley. And in fact it was the Romans who built the first road up to the outpost, which was later to be used as the foundation for the present *mulattiera*.

During the Middle Ages, when warfare between neighbouring villages was commonplace, Sommocolonia was a *Comune* in its own right. Sommocolonia then became a fortified village completely surrounded by defensive walls. In 1532 it was incorporated into the *Comune* of Barga after being defeated by overwhelming forces of a 'Barga-Medicean' alliance.

Originally, there were two towers but only one had survived over the years. The *Rocca* was the inner fortified keep. The village was further protected by another defensive wall all around its perimeter. So the *Rocca* was in fact an inner bastion, which could withstand a long period of siege. It even had its own well of fresh water. It was rumoured that from the *Rocca* there was a secret tunnel, which led to an exit half way down the mountain. This provided a last minute means of escape in case the inner defences were in danger of being breached. No one has ever discovered this secret tunnel and its existence has always been a constant source of speculation.

The construction of the present tower and the fortifications of the village are commonly attributed to Countess Matilda. Over the years the tower suffered a fair amount of damage during the earthquakes of 1902 and 1920. However, the tower was so strongly built that it remained almost intact up until the Second World War. It was during the battle in December 1944 that it was irrevocably damaged and ended up in the present state of ruin.

The 1902 earthquake was a very severe one, which caused quite a lot of damage in the village. The emotional impact it had on the inhabitants can be attested by a poem composed by the village poet at the time. (See Appendix).

The only gateway into the fortified settlement can clearly be seen in an illustration of the village dating back to 1500. The road leading to the gateway or *Porta* is the old Roman road or modern *mulattiera*. Even to this day the area where the mule track reaches the outskirts of the village is known as *La Porta* (The Gateway).

Now that the village shop included a bar, I started frequenting this café to sit and watch the men playing cards and of course scrounge the odd *cicca* whenever possible.

Prior to this, I used to go from time to time to the *Dopolavoro*. I was really too young to frequent the *Dopolavoro* but nobody seemed to object. I think that they probably felt sorry for me because I did not have a father figure at home.

If I was lucky one of the men would treat me to a *magnese*, a fizzy drink. This *magnese* was concocted by pouring a sachet of white crystals into a glass of water. It would fizz up very quickly. I can only compare the fizzy action of this drink to the modern "Andrew's Liver Salts". The *magnese* had a slightly sweet taste and it made a very pleasant non-alcoholic drink.

The *Dopolavoro* was in fact the only rendezvous where men could go to relax after work. Playing cards was their main recreational activity. They would normally play for the price of a glass of the cheap local wine.

A very popular game among the men was one called *La Morra*. This game was for two players. They would quickly thrust forward an arm showing one or more extended fingers whilst at the same time shouting out a number between 2 and 10. The object of the game was to guess the total number of fingers shown by the hands of the two players. A correct guess would score one point. Competitors would declare before the commencement of the game how many points had to be scored in order to win.

The game would be conducted at a phenomenal speed, the competitors literally rattling off their guesses like the 'rat-tat-tat' of a machine gun. At times it would be so fast that a non-expert bystander would have great difficulty discerning how many fingers had been shown. To a young boy it was practically impossible. The competitors on the other hand had no difficulty at all and whenever one of them scored a point there would be a quick pause before continuing with the game at the same breakneck speed.

Another pastime, which was indulged in rather less frequently, was the *stornello*. *Stornelli* were popular songs particularly common in Central Italy. These songs were composed of two hendecasyllabic lines, preceded by one pentasyllabic line. The first and last lines would rhyme. They were somewhat similar to modern calypsos, in that they were spontaneously composed each time.

Whenever there was a *gara* (contest) between two *stornellatori*, one of the contestants would start off by singing about a recent event regarding his opponent. The latter would answer him with a suitable *stornello* of his own. And so the contest would continue back and forth until one of the two contestants ran out of ideas. Sometimes a *stornellata* (a *stornello* contest) might go on for hours.

The *Dopolavoro* was situated at the other end of the village and on dark winter nights when I walked home, often alone, along the unlit streets, I used to whistle and sing to bolster my spirits and give me courage. I tried to kid myself that I wasn't frightened but I was always glad when I reached home safely.

The new café meant that there were now two meeting places in the village. In the evenings the café would get quite busy. The men would play cards, the losers usually paying for the wine. One of the regulars was a chap called Ilario Bertagna. He was really quite a comic and he often had people in stitches with his dry humour.

Everyone would look forward to his arrival each evening and they would shout: "*Ecco Ilario*," (here comes Ilario) for he was always a constant source of amusement. What made him even funnier was the fact that he uttered his witticisms with a dead pan face.

One evening, he arrived up at the café at the usual time, went in and without saying a word started to look under the tables. Bemused, one of the men said to him: *"Cosa cercate Ilario?"* (What are you looking for Ilario?) Without batting an eyelid he replied: *"Ieri sera ho perso cinque lire. Non saranno caso mai per terra?"* (Last night I lost five lire. I was wondering whether they might be lying somewhere on the floor.) He had lost the five lire playing cards the previous evening. The joke was a little too subtle for the others to immediately comprehend but when they did eventually understand it, the room erupted in hoots of laughter.

Ilario was also a great picker of raspberries and mushrooms. He would frequently set off with another chap called Ferruccio, who lived in the *piazza San Rocco*. In the summer they would go picking wild raspberries. They would go up into the thickets of the lower slopes of the Apuan Alps.

Sometimes they would stay away for two or three days, after which they would return with baskets full of raspberries. With these raspberries they would make a cordial which would last them all winter. At mushroom time they would set off again looking for *funghi porcini* (ceps). Again they would be away two or three days on end and invariably return laden with sacks full of mushrooms. A few of the mushrooms would be eaten fresh but most of them were for drying.

The mushrooms would be sliced and placed on a board to dry in the sun. Dried mushrooms were, and still are, a very profitable cash crop. Every able-bodied person in the village would go looking for mushrooms but nobody had the expertise of Ilario and Ferruccio. They knew the spots where the mushrooms grew and they would never reveal them to anyone else.

I remember in the autumn of 1943 going looking for mushrooms with a group of people from the village. Because of my irrational fear of snakes I would never venture far into the woodlands on my own.

We walked in the direction of Lama for about thirty minutes and came across a section of woodland, which had been partly felled. The branches were still lying on the ground and covered in a carpet of undisturbed leaves. Someone in our group started lifting some of the branches and suddenly he gave a whoop of joy for there in front of him was a veritable spread of mushrooms ready for the picking. We all started to lift up various branches and sure enough there were literally loads of mushrooms.

It's a real pleasure when you come across something like this. We were lucky because we had stumbled on a patch where no one else had been. We all returned with our baskets full of mushrooms.

I had from time to time found the occasional mushroom whenever I had wandered a few yards off the trodden paths but this was the first and only time that I had been able to find and pick a whole basketful. The feeling of elation is really something to be experienced.

What a wonderful sight it was to see all the boards covered with mushrooms drying in the early autumn sun. This was the time of year when other products would also be put out to dry: tomatoes for homemade tomato puree, *borlotti* beans for winter soups, and cobs of sweet corn. When dry, the sweet corn would be removed from the cobs and the grains milled into flour. This flour was the basis for another type of *polenta*, the so-called *polenta gialla* (yellow polenta). *Polenta gialla* was definitely more palatable than *polenta* made with chestnut flour. It was not often eaten because maize flour was fairly expensive in comparison to the plentiful chestnut flour.

Autumn was also the time when lots of fruit were in season. The small red figs were particularly delicious. The first time I came across a tree laden with figs I ate till I was full: I wouldn't be surprised if I ate thirty or more figs. They were lovely and ripe and the centres were sweet like jam. I spent most of the next day going to the toilet. After that I ensured that I was more moderate in my intake of figs.

The particular fruit that I did not like were persimmons. There was a persimmon tree growing at the side of the path, which led to the cemetery. I found them very bitter and after trying them a couple of times I never tasted them again. Their bitterness may have been because they were probably not ripe. I wonder whether 2000 feet above sea level was perhaps not too high for them to ripen properly.

This would probably explain why this persimmon tree was always laden with unpicked fruit. Another unusual fruit were medlars. These need to be very ripe and mushy (almost rotten) before they can be enjoyed. Otherwise they can be very bitter.

Our neighbour Mr Vincenti had a long garden at the front of his house, which ran all along the edge of the road as far as our house. In this garden there were some beautiful pear trees. In the autumn, they would be literally laden with lovely big pears, and I always looked at them with covetous eyes. In between these pear trees there were beehives, about five or six in total. Mr Vincenti was the only person in the village who dabbled in apiculture.

The bees would swarm in May and as the garden was just outside our front door, it was exciting to watch the bees swarming and wonder where they were going to settle. Sometimes the swarm would take off and disappear in the distance never to be seen again but mostly they would settle on a nearby tree.

Although he kept bees for the honey, Mr Vincenti did not have the expertise to deal with swarming bees. For this task he had to call on another villager, Mr Biondi, who was a kind of jack of all trades. Mr Biondi would come along carrying a special utensil for smoking out the bees. He would don a mask to protect his face and proceed to use his smoke gun until he had enticed the queen into a container.

Sometimes he might have to shake or even saw off a branch in order to cause the queen to fall. Once he had captured the queen bee he would deposit her into an empty hive. After that all the other bees would follow the queen into the new hive and a new colony was thus formed. I always marvelled at Mr Biondi and I looked upon him as a very courageous man.

A chap called Cascianella, who lived at the southern end of the village, had teamed up with my uncle Fiore and they had started supplying meat off ration. They would hike all the way over the Apuan Alps into Emilia Romagna and smuggle the odd contraband animal into the village. Arriving back in Sommocolonia they would slaughter this beast in Cascianella's stable. After cutting up the beast, the various joints and cuts of meat would be offered for sale to the villagers at a slightly increased price. In this way we were able to purchase extra food and eat meat a little more frequently.

Everyone was grateful for this service. The contraband activities of these two men lasted about four months. As happens in most communities there was someone in the village who either disliked them or was jealous of their clandestine business enterprise. The authorities had been anonymously informed and the *carabinieri* (police) came up to the village to investigate. They arrested both men and took them away for questioning. After a couple of days they released them through lack of incriminating evidence but this put paid to the plentiful supply of fresh meat.

Another service provided by these two 'entrepreneurs' was that they had established a system for the bartering of goods. In Emilia Romagna, beyond the Apuan Alps, there was a surplus of potatoes and in our area there was an abundance of chestnut flour. The bartering arrangement was two sacks of potatoes for one sack of chestnut flour. The potatoes formed a natural accompaniment to the meat and for a short while we had enough food to fill our bellies.

The village was a very tightly knit community and over the years there had been a lot of intermarriage. Constant intermarrying can result in periodic instances of idiocy. I remember one family who lived in the *piazza S. Rocco*. They had a son called Bruno, who had been certified insane. He was normally confined in the *manicomio* (mental asylum) in Lucca.

On one occasion Bruno was allowed to come and stay, on leave, with his parents in Sommocolonia. The whole village was apprehensive and they were constantly talking about how dangerous Bruno was. When he returned to the asylum at the end of his short leave, everyone breathed a sigh of relief. I saw him once and he certainly struck me as very odd, for he had a most frightening vacant look in his eyes.

Aunt Dora had managed to get a job working for the Cosimini family. Mr Cosimini ran a grain and seed merchants business in Barga. He was consequently quite well off. His bride was a member of the Passerotti family from Sommocolonia.

Mrs Cosimini was looking for help in the home because she had a young child of eighteen months and was expecting another. They had previously engaged one or two different girls but they had all been unsatisfactory.

Then one day Mrs Cosimini asked Aunt Dora if she would like to help. Dora was a more mature person, and therefore more reliable. Besides she was also a relative. Dora saw this as a way of not only earning some badly needed money but of also being able to help her own family. After working in the house for some months, she was asked to also help out in the business.

At Dora's request, I would pop in from time to time on my way home from school and she would load me up with any surplus food that the Cosimini family did not want.

In September 1943, came the news that Italy had capitulated. An armistice was signed on the third of September and we all thought that the war was now over. Most Italians had the same idea and they began to celebrate. One of their first actions was to open up all the POW and internment camps under their jurisdiction and allow the prisoners to go free.

Suddenly, we found that many foodstuffs that had been unavailable during the previous three years were now back in the shops. Most notable among these was the reappearance of parmesan cheese. Everybody was talking about it and saying that this proved that the fascists had been hoarding all these foodstuffs and keeping them for their own personal consumption.

We were soon to be disillusioned, for our newfound freedom was not to last long. It took the Germans only a few days to establish their domain over central and northern Italy. And so in no time at all, the whole area of Italy, which had not been liberated by the Allies, became an occupied country under the domination of the German Reich. The luxury foodstuffs soon disappeared from the shops and rationing got even stricter than before. We were now to experience a period of even greater hardships.

The king had ordered that Mussolini be arrested in order to sign the armistice. He was therefore imprisoned but the Germans soon freed him. Mussolini then declared a new republic, the 'Italian Social Republic' or the republic of '*Salò*' as it came to be known. He lived in northern Italy until his eventual capture and execution by the Italian partisans in 1945.

A new corps of neo-fascists had been formed who were known as the '*Brigata Nera Mussolini*'. These popinjays would wander the streets strutting like peacocks in their new uniforms. They were armed and they were merciless towards anyone who criticised the new regime.

These neo-fascists went round asserting their newly acquired authority everywhere. Fortunately they did not come up to Sommocolonia. Perhaps the trek on foot was below their dignity. In the Barga area they started looking for suitable buildings that might be utilised as garages. Then they began combing the area for motorcars and lorries.

In this respect they had very little luck because the Germans had already beaten them to it. Besides, those few people who did possess a motor vehicle, had suddenly made them disappear as if by magic. In the private garage of one of the doctors they did find a motor car but it had no tyres. In a rage they dragged it out of the garage and hauled it away on its metal wheels.

The '*Brigata Nera*' then decided to hunt for radio sets with the excuse that too many people were listening to the BBC broadcasts from London. They did have a little success at first because they took the people completely by surprise.

Some of them were so fanatical that they often had to be restrained by the German military. Most of these 'little Hitlers' became marked men and at the end of the war they paid a heavy penalty for their allegiance to the deposed dictator.

Meanwhile, all the newly freed POWs and internees were trying to make their way down to the allied lines in southern Italy. Some were recaptured by the Germans but many managed to wend their way down through the Apennines on their journey south. They soon started trickling through our village in groups of two or three. They came dressed in all manner of clothing: some in full military uniform, some with mixed military and civilian clothes and others dressed as peasants.

There were people of many different nationalities and one or two even arrived on horseback. They would be fed and given a bed for a night or two until they went off again rested and refreshed. This trickle of foreign ex prisoners and internees lasted for several weeks.

A very well planned escape route had been organised by the clergy. In our area the main helper was the parish priest of Tiglio, a village not far from Sommocolonia. He was in fact responsible for saving many allied POWs. He was lucky that he was not found out for the penalty for helping or harbouring allied personnel was invariably death.

Now that I was going down to Barga everyday in school time, I was given the task to call in at the bakers in Barga and buy the bread. Buying straight from the bakery was always a few *centesimi* cheaper and we badly needed to save every *centesimo* we could.

Orlando and I had grown a bit sick of the usual walk back to Sommocolonia. We had now found a different route. We would wander up the banks of the *Corsonna* river until we reached a little footbridge known as *La Passerella*. It was a very flimsy bridge made of wood planking and the sides were two thick metal wires stretching from one bank to the other. We used to love jumping up and down while crossing this bridge.

One day in April 1944, when this flimsy bridge was swinging very heavily in response to our tomfoolery, the ration books, which had been stuck into the top of the satchel slung across my shoulders, fell out into the river. On seeing this, my first thought was to get the ration books back. I jumped into the river to try and retrieve them.

I had not realised that the river was quite swollen because of recent rain and to my great consternation I found myself being dragged away by the current. Fortunately, Orlando came running after me and managed to drag me back ashore. I never recovered the ration books but Orlando had repaid his debt to me: it was he who had saved me this time.

I was in an awful state because not only was I absolutely drenched but what was I going to tell Mother? When I got home and recounted what had happened I immediately got a good hiding for being so careless. Then Mother relented and felt sorry for me when she realised what danger I had been in.

Pietrino, the part time civil servant advised her to go down to the *Comune* and explain the position. He was sure that we would qualify for an emergency issue of ration books.

The next day Mother went down to Barga to the *Comune* and related what had happened. At this the civil servant in charge of issuing ration books retorted: "*Signora non c' è niente da fare. Bisogna stringere la cintola.*" (Madam we can't help you. You'll just have to tighten your belts.)

What were we going to do without any ration books? The villagers were very good to us. Many of them rallied round and helped us by sharing a little of their rations with us. It was also fortunate that there was only a week to go to the end of the month and the next issue of ration cards.

At the end of the war, Mother made a point of going down to the *Comune* in Barga and confronting this petty little official about his cavalier attitude in respect of the matter of the lost ration books. She publicly remonstrated with him, ensuring that everyone around clearly heard her. In reply the arrogant council official just hung his head in shame and did not utter a word.

Chapter 12

In the spring of that year, squadrons of American Flying Fortresses (B-17s) began flying over the village heading north. Every day, there was a deafening drone of aircraft in the air. In the morning they headed north with their lethal cargo of bombs. They would return late afternoon on their way back to base. They would fly in formations of five or six abreast so numerous that it took well over an hour for them all to fly past.

They were obviously on their way to carpet bomb some part of Germany and our thoughts were "God help those poor people at the receiving end of those bombs". Once or twice, the odd bomber that had been unable to reach its target through some malfunction would return early, shedding its bomb load at random on its way back.

One day in May when Orlando and I we were returning home from school we heard a plane which was flying a lot lower than normal. All of a sudden there were loud explosions quite nearby which frightened us out of our wits: the plane had released its bombs in order to lighten its load for a quick return to base. The two of us decided that we had better get off the main road and that day we made our way home through fields and woodlands.

It was also about this time that allied planes began to bomb the metallurgical works at Fornaci. The allies had obviously learnt that it had been converted into a munitions factory. Fornaci lay in a very narrow valley between some high mountains and bombing it was a very tricky operation. I gather that some bombs did eventually find their target causing a considerable amount of damage.

The allies were getting nearer day by day. In the evening we would often see the glare of explosions behind the mountains to the west of us. They had started to bomb the coastal fortifications of the port of La Spezia and the neighbouring area.

All of us were constantly enquiring about the progress of the approaching allied troops. Each night the men would sit round the radio set in the *Dopolavoro* listening to the latest news.

Great excitement towards the end of June. We had learnt that the allies had now reached Cecina, just south of Livorno. This was Tuscan territory and it would soon be our turn to greet the liberating army. Unfortunately, their advance suddenly came to a temporary halt.

During the month of July there was a lot of allied aircraft activity in the Serchio valley. Their main target was the munitions factory at Fornaci. In contrast the month of August was relatively calm. The only sound of aircraft came from the flying Fortresses on their way to Germany.

Meanwhile the allies had started to advance again. They had now crossed the river Arno in several places. At the beginning of September they had captured Pisa and were heading for Lucca. God willing it wouldn't be long now.

The German army had become an occupying force with the consequence that the Italian population were treated as enemies. They began to arrest all the able bodied men who were not members of the new "*Brigata Nera*". They did this by means of the *rastrellamento*, a systematic form of roundup.

There were very few Germans stationed in the region of the upper Serchio valley. They would therefore bring in special troops, target a specific town or village by surrounding it, then comb through all the buildings apprehending every able bodied man they found. All prisoners would then be transported to Germany to work as slave labour in camps and factories.

There was always plenty of warning regarding the Germans arriving and all the men in Barga would escape up into the mountains. Some of them fled in our direction and their first refuge was Sommocolonia. If ever there was any danger of the Germans venturing up to the village, the men would then run off into the higher mountains.

A very clever system of communication had been devised to warn people of the possible arrival in Sommocolonia of German soldiers.

From the terrace of the priest's house there was a wonderful view of the valley below. The road leading from Barga to Ponte di Catagnana, at the bottom of the mountain was clearly visible. If the Germans by any chance decided to head into our mountains, the women at Ponte di Catagnana would hang out white bed sheets in a particular pattern.

If this were to happen, the men would then go and hide further up into the higher slopes well above Sommocolonia. There was a chap called Mozzino in the village who was well into his sixties. He had nothing to fear because the Germans were looking for younger men. And yet, he would wander off with his thirteen-year-old grandson and hide in the mountains with all the other men.

If you asked him why he was running away, intimating that he was too old, he would reply: "I'm just going to keep my grandson Giovanni company." And if you asked his grandson, he would reply: "I'm just going to keep my grandfather company."

In actual fact, the Germans only ever came up to Sommocolonia twice during their roundup raids. Each time all they could find were women and children. After that, they obviously decided that it was not worth the effort of climbing all the way up to the village for nothing. These early warning systems worked so well that the Germans were never able to capture any able bodied men from our village during their roundups in our area.

One man who unfortunately found himself surrounded in Barga during one of the German roundups decided to climb a pine tree to hide. A group of German soldiers chose to sit under that very tree to have a meal. The poor fellow had to remain very still in the tree without making a sound for nearly two hours until the troops below decided to move on.

Another person, who had been captured in Barga, managed to escape by jumping from the train on his way to northern Italy. He landed rather heavily and broke his ankle but he at least avoided being transported off to Germany. Most of the men who were captured in this way never returned after the war.

For about two or three months the village was milling with many extra people from Barga. They would all speculate and discuss about the progress of the war and it was really quite exciting. Some of them had decided that they would bide their time up in the mountains and so they brought bedding and spare clothes with them.

With so many extra inhabitants in the village, several *barghigiani* (inhabitants of Barga) had to sleep rough in barns and stables. They did not mind for it was better than being captured by the Germans.

It was at this time that I got caught up in a bit of a contretemps with a boy called Bruno. Bruno was about the same age as me and he normally lived in Lucca. He was a grandson of Ferruccio the mushroom expert. I particularly remember his father because he always wore a long thick leather glove on one arm. Apparently he had been in some kind of industrial accident and had lost his hand. He must have had a prosthetic hand because he never took his glove off.

During the summer Bruno's family would often come up to Sommocolonia for a short stay in order to get away from the stifling heat of the city. Bruno was rather arrogant and he considered himself a cut above us *montanari* (hillbillies) in Sommocolonia. For some reason he had taken a particular dislike to me and he was always passing snide remarks about me.

That summer Bruno's family had moved out of Lucca for safety. One day Bruno really needled me. This led to unpleasant words being exchanged between us and the outcome was that he challenged me to a fight. Some of the men from Barga decided that it should be done properly with boxing gloves.

On the day of the fight the *piazza* was packed with onlookers. I had no knowledge of boxing and I naively kept on the defence all the time. To my shame I ended up being well and truly beaten.

After the fight, a young man called Mario, who was a nephew of my uncle Joe (Aunt Dora's husband), suggested that I ought to have a *rivincita* (return match). I had never been bellicose by nature, and I certainly had no desire to receive another hiding. Mario kept insisting and said to me: "Don't worry Bernard. I'll teach you how to box."

The return match was arranged for a week later. During the intervening period Mario gave me lots of practice in boxing. He explained that I had been beaten during the previous fight because I had remained constantly on the defensive. His strategy for winning this time was that I should attack rather than defend.

On the day of the *rivincita* there were even more people assembled in the *piazza* to watch the 'great match'. On the advice of Mario, I changed my tactics and went straight onto the offensive, taking Bruno completely by surprise. After a few well-landed punches by me, Bruno announced that he had had enough and I was declared the winner to the great delight of all my pals in the village. Nowadays, over fifty years later, Bruno and I always have a good laugh whenever we reminisce about this incident.

Late August a small troop of German soldiers (about a dozen in all) came up to Sommocolonia. They laid down telephone wires connecting the village to Barga. We were all speculating whether they had come to establish some kind of observation post.

But they were not to stay long. About ten days later they packed up and left and everyone was wondering why they had suddenly gone. It transpired later that the axis troops had decided to entrench themselves in Lama, which was the next mountain above Sommocolonia. Lama certainly offered a better commanding position for defence purposes.

Meanwhile the allied advance north was slowly but inexorably continuing. Their progress was not quick enough for us because we would have liked them to manoeuvre a sudden speedy repulse of the enemy and free us once and for all.

The Germans operated a type of razed earth policy, which consisted of destroying, as far as possible, all lines of communication behind them when retreating. This meant blowing up all road bridges and railway lines.

Consequently they blew up all the bridges over the river Arno. Despite this vandalistic policy, somewhat reminiscent of the early barbarian invasions of Italy, they spared one bridge: the famous Ponte

Vecchio in Florence. Many theories have been put forward as to the reason for this. Whatever it was, it is indeed fortunate that this beautiful, unique medieval bridge was mercifully saved.

An amusing story is told of an incident on the Ponte Vecchio during the Middle Ages. At that time, the present day shops were occupied by moneylenders and moneychangers. As such they did not have any merchandise on display or for sale. One day a peasant wandered into the city for the first time. On reaching the Ponte Vecchio he became very inquisitive as to the purpose of all the empty premises.

He then entered one of the business premises and enquired of the proprietor: "Excuse me sir. But can you tell me what it is that you sell here?" Florentines are renowned for their love of wanting to amuse themselves at other people's expense. The moneylender saw this as a wonderful opportunity to make fun of the ignorant peasant and replied: "We sell donkeys' heads, my good man!" The peasant may have been ignorant of the facts but he was very astute. Quick as a flash he retorted: "I can see that you have been very busy sir, for there remains only one of them for sale!"

We were soon to learn that the Germans had started blowing up all the bridges along the *Serchio* valley. Once again they spared one bridge. This was the *Ponte della Maddalena* at Borgo a Mozzano.

This bridge is a narrow humped back bridge with asymmetrical arches. It was first built around about the eleventh century and took on its present shape in the thirteenth century. It is a classic example of a medieval packhorse bridge. As it was very narrow it was obviously of no strategic military importance. The German Officers in charge of demolishing the bridges must have realised its historical importance and left it standing.

Although the correct name of this packhorse bridge is *Ponte della Maddalena*, it is commonly known as *Ponte del Diavolo* (the Devil's Bridge). The legend goes that when the bridge was built in the Middle Ages the authorities entrusted the work to a master builder in the region. They arranged for the bridge to be finished by a certain date, stipulating draconian penalties for a late finish. Half way through the task the builder realised that owing to a series of unforeseen delays he would not be able to finish the bridge by the allocated date. It is here that he turned to the devil for help.

The devil agreed to help him on one condition: that he must have the soul of the first creature across the completed bridge. The builder agreed but he was also a crafty Tuscan peasant. No sooner had he finished building the bridge than he herded a pig across it. Thus the devil was thwarted in his attempt to gain a human soul and had to be content with the soul of a pig. And so to this day this bridge is commonly known as 'The Devil's Bridge'.

In July, Nella Saporiti, my mother's step aunt, who lived in Lucca, came to stay with us in Sommocolonia to get away from the enervating heat of the city. She stayed all summer and she eventually got stranded so that she remained in the village right throughout the front line.

She may also have thought that she would be safer up in the mountains. If only she could have known what was going to happen. Fortunately, she managed to survive all the dangers of the front line unscathed.

Everyone was now getting really impatient with the allies. They seemed to be taking such an age to reach us. Were we ever going to be liberated?

Then, towards the end of September, the Germans began mining all the bridges in the Barga region. On the morning of Tuesday 26th September the German commander ordered the Provost of Barga, Monsignor Lombardi, to be ready to ring the church bells to warn the population to stay clear of the area around all the bridges.

There would be a time lag of approximately 30 to 40 minutes between the ringing of the bells and the destruction of the bridges. This would allow the people who lived near the bridges, plenty of time to escape to safety.

At 1 pm the order arrived for the bells to be rung. Suddenly all the church bells in Barga began to ring. They were not ringing in jubilation for they were intoning the slow cadence of the death knell. We all knew what this knoll meant and it was a most appropriate omen of impending disaster.

At approximately two o' clock in the afternoon there was a very loud rumble and we now realised that the bridges were gone. In Barga there were two parallel bridges. The second one had always been regarded as just a very wide footbridge. Nevertheless this bridge was also destroyed.

There now followed a period of uncertainty. The German troops were still lingering about in the area, as attested by the frequent detonation of mines all along the railway line from Lucca.

We entered a short period when we seemed to be in a sort of no mans land. The Germans had gone and the allies had not yet arrived. Would the partisans take over the region?

At the beginning of October we started to hear shelling focused on the area round Fornaci and Barga. This time it was definitely the allied troops who were advancing. We had been waiting for this for a very long time and it hardly seemed true.

With a bit of luck it would only be a short time before we were really liberated. Two days later the forward elements of the allied troops finally arrived in Barga.

Mother and Dora were looking forward to being able to talk to someone in English. It was now over four years since we had been absent from the UK and, for obvious reasons no one had dared speak in English during that time. I remember Mother saying: "God willing the war will soon be a thing of the past for us. Our troubles will at last be over and we will shortly be returning home."

What irony indeed, for we were now on the threshold of a long precarious period of life in the frontline, with all its concomitant dangers. The famous *Linea Gotica* (Gothic Line) was to halt right at our village for several months.

Chapter 13

B efore the Germans began their retreat from the area, they proceeded to spread all kinds of scurrilous propaganda about the allied troops. The most scandalous of these rumours were in respect of the American soldiers. They stated that there were many black soldiers among them who were still very primitive. A lot of them were cannibals and they particularly loved to eat little children.

Enlightened and educated Italians treated these scare-mongering lies with the scorn and contempt they deserved. Most of the villagers, on the other hand, were quite ignorant and rather gullible. They tended to believe, in their own ingenuous way, these ridiculous stories. Whereas they had previously been looking forward to being liberated by the allies, they now began to feel rather apprehensive about being overrun by 'cannibals'.

At the beginning of October the allied troops finally arrived in Barga. We had all been looking forward to welcoming British and/or American soldiers. To our astonishment they turned out to be Brazilians. They were members of the Brazilian Expeditionary Force who formed part of the allied armies. I don't think many people knew about the fact that Brazilian troops were fighting with the allied forces during World War Two. In fact, whenever I have since recounted this to friends and colleagues in later years, I have invariably been met with looks of incredulity.

Because of the dangers of the frontline situation, all the schools in the Barga area had been closed and they did not open again during that academic year. This in effect marked the end of my schooling in the *Scuola Media*. When the school authorities announced that the schools would not be opening that October, all the schoolchildren were, not unnaturally, delighted at the prospect of an extended 'holiday' from schoolwork.

Prior to the Brazilian troops arriving in Sommocolonia, the weather had been absolutely atrocious. It had been raining constantly for two days with terrible thunderstorms. October always tended to be rather a wet month but that year it turned out to be the wettest October for many years.

Early during the second night a thunderbolt, attracted by the lightning conductor on the campanile, had struck the ground nearby with such force that the whole village was awakened by it. The noise was quite deafening and everyone thought that a bomb had been dropped. We were all very apprehensive and spent a restless night, expecting more bombs.

It was not till the following morning that we learnt what had happened. We went to have a look to see if there was any damage. The thunderbolt had discharged into the road just below *Nonno* Bonafede's house. And there in the centre of the road was a sizeable hole.

The next day it rained on and off for most of the day. We went to bed that night half-fearing that we might experience another thunderbolt or two. If a powerful thunderbolt were to directly hit a house it could certainly cause quite a bit of damage. There were no thunderbolts but what did in fact happen, turned out to be much more harmful for our family.

The Brazilians had mistakenly assumed that the Germans were occupying Sommocolonia and they had decided to target the village with artillery fire.

It was round about midnight when they started their shelling of the village. All of a sudden we experienced an almighty explosion. Incredibly, one of the first shells managed to hit our house. The shell went clean through the stone wall on the eastern side of the house and whistled right through our bedroom. Fortunately the shell had found the window on the opposite wall and, after smashing through it, went careering out into the street below.

My mother, Aldo, and I were all asleep in the double bed. Mother normally slept with her arm around my baby brother Aldo and I slept at the foot of the bed. I had always been a very heavy sleeper and that night, although I felt the whole house tremble, my thoughts were that it was only another thunderbolt and I just turned over to go back to sleep again.

A few seconds later my aunt Dora and Nella, who were sleeping in the other bedroom, entered our room in their nightclothes in order to find out what had happened. They were both rather startled and shaken by the noise of the shell hitting the house. Dora carried a candle and it was very difficult to make things out clearly in the dim candlelight. Also the air in the room was full of dust. The bed had been badly damaged by the blast and there was a large stone on the side of the bed below the windowsill.

It took us some time to realise the full extent of the damage. Mother was lying with Aldo in her arms. Aldo's face was completely covered in blood and everyone thought he had been killed. On further inspection it became clear that it was Mother who was bleeding from a deep gash in her forehead. Thus Mother became the first person to be wounded in the village.

We all began to get dressed as quickly as we could, grabbed some protective outer garments and made our way to Mr Vincenti's, the nearest house, for help. The weather was dreadful; the rain was pelting down and we got completely drenched just running the few yards between the two houses.

At the Vincenti's house they were very kind and helpful. They proceeded to clean Mother's wound and bandage it as best possible. Mr Vincenti said we could sleep in the hayloft next to the house.

My first thoughts were that this was going to be quite a comfortable place to spend the night. Shortly after settling down in the hay we heard little creatures scuttling around. It was then that we realised that the loft was swarming with rats. I don't think we slept that night for fear of these horrid creatures. So we kept awake and vigilant in order to make sure that we would not be bitten by them. We were indeed very grateful when dawn began to break.

The next day brought another problem. Mother required urgent medical attention and she really needed to go down to the hospital in

Barga. She tried to get someone in the village to accompany her to the hospital but was unable to find anyone willing to help. Everyone kept saying that it would be too dangerous to venture down to Barga.

Rumours were rife: the Germans might try to retaliate and shell the Brazilian positions in Barga. Or they might even try to recapture the town. Everyone was speculating as to the dangers and offering advice. Mother was undaunted by all this talk of danger. Besides she needed to go and get expert medical help. So, very bravely, she set off fairly early in the morning to walk down to the hospital on her own.

Later that morning we started getting worried about Mother's safety. We could see and hear that Barga was being shelled by the Germans. Had she made it to the hospital or had she become a casualty of this new artillery raid? When we saw Mother reappear late afternoon we were greatly relieved.

She had quite a story to tell. First of all there was the difficulty of crossing the *Corsonna* river at *Ponte di Catagnana* because the Germans had blown up the bridge. This meant that she had to walk upstream and cross the river by the precarious *Passerella*. Although it had stopped raining she had to be extremely careful not to slip.

When she arrived in Barga she found that the two bridges had also been destroyed. The Brazilian troops had constructed a temporary footbridge and mother had to negotiate this flimsy bridge with great care. No sooner had she crossed the bridge than the Germans began to shell the town. She had to dive into the nearest house for shelter. The artillery barrage lasted most of the morning.

As soon as there was a lull in the shelling she ventured out, grabbed hold of one of the Brazilian soldiers and asked him to accompany her to the hospital. He was reluctant at first but Mother kept insisting and he finally agreed. He had accompanied her for only a short way when the shelling suddenly started again. Once more, Mother had to seek shelter in the nearest house. She then grabbed another soldier who accompanied her on a further stretch of the journey.

And so between several bouts of shelling and with the help of various soldiers, she was able to make her way to the hospital where her wound was medicated and re-bandaged. She was then given an anti tetanus injection and was told that, as it was quite a deep wound, it would need to be treated every day if possible, or at least every other day.

The shelling had been quite extensive and it transpired that there had been several casualties, both wounded and dead, among the civilian population. One story was told of an elderly lady who had literally been 'splattered' against a solid wooden door by the force of a blast.

On the return journey Mother had to re-negotiate the two footbridges all on her own. She seemed quite cheerful considering the ordeal she had been through but she was dreading the idea of having to keep going down to the hospital every day, a not inconsiderable distance to walk even at the best of times. Under the threat of constant shelling this represented quite a problem.

She needn't have worried for the matter was soon to resolve itself. The Brazilians had at last realised that there were no Germans at all in the village and the following day they arrived en masse to occupy Sommocolonia. We had at last been 'liberated'!

The nearest German troops were in Lama, the next mountain ridge above Sommocolonia. In fact it turned out that they had dug themselves in quite deeply and were obviously prepared for a long stand off.

Now that the allied troops had arrived in Sommocolonia, the Brazilian medical personnel treated Mother's head wound on a daily basis. The wound was quite deep but they medicated it with penicillin powder, a wonderful new drug at the time. In fact it was so effective that within a short time the wound stopped suppurating and began to dry up and heal.

The day the Brazilians arrived many of us boys went to the *piazza* to watch them unload the mule train which had brought up their supplies. The Brazilians, unlike their American allies, were completely integrated and they displayed no racial discrimination whatsoever in their ranks. In fact most of them were coloured and obviously of mixed race.

I remember one of them who was really black. He was a chubby little chap with a rotund face. He was the very epitome of cheerfulness for he was always smiling. He stripped to the waist and despite the rather cold October weather proceeded to wash himself under the ice cold water of the fountain in the *piazza*. All the while he was singing and whistling.

The Brazilians established their Headquarters in one of the houses in the *piazza*. In front of the house, which had previously been the village shop, they had installed a machine gun post. This was an ideal spot because it afforded a commanding view of the two northern entrances to the *piazza*. Our lengthy period of life in the front line proper had now begun.

Chapter 14

Two days after the arrival of the Brazilian troops a small reconnoitring patrol of Germans ventured into the village square. When they saw the machine gun emplacement, which for some strange reason was unmanned at that particular time, they quickly retreated via the back of the *Castello*. All this time, Don Fredianelli, the parish priest who had been making a pastoral visit to one of the houses in the *piazza*, had observed them.

No sooner had the Germans left, than Berto Biondi, a villager who had recently joined the partisans, came into the square. He was a bit nonplussed at first when he saw the silent gesticulations of the priest who was trying to warn him of the German patrol.

As soon as the priest mouthed the word *Tedeschi*, Berto immediately understood and asked: "*dove?*" When the priest pointed in the direction of the retreating Germans, Berto ingenuously went running after them letting off a few rounds of his Sten gun. Fortunately for Berto the Germans had by now disappeared for he would certainly have been well outgunned had it culminated in a shoot-out.

After this incident the Brazilians made sure that all their machine gun posts were manned at all times. They also posted sentries in various spots to guard all the northern entrances to the village.

The Germans now began to shell the village every day and we were to experience the daily life of hell in the frontline. Their artillery raids followed no specific pattern. Each raid would consist of anything up to a dozen shells and last about ten minutes.

The shelling would be at sporadic times of the day: sometimes once, sometimes twice and even three or more times a day. Whenever the Germans started shelling, we would all dive for cover into the nearest house and shelter ourselves as best as possible.

Because our house at *Monticino* had been damaged in the first artillery raid on the village we had to move into another house in the village. Besides, our old house was in a very exposed spot and as such represented a wide-open target for the German artillery. We went to live in Wanda's house, which was situated in a fairly sheltered spot next to the main church.

Now that we experienced the daily shelling by the Germans, we all took to sleeping in the basements of our houses for greater safety. It was also more practical; during the daytime we could easily seek immediate shelter at the first sign of an artillery raid but at night when we were asleep it would have been rather difficult.

And so, our family ended up sleeping in the basement of *Nonno* Bonafede's house, which was situated next to the church of *San Frediano*.

This basement was a very large room with high ceilings and an earth floor. All round were wooden slatted shelves, which were raised about two-foot off the ground. They made ideal dormitory beds, and we slept in this basement for the whole of our time in the frontline.

In all there were eighteen of us sleeping in that large basement room: my aunt Rosina's family (six) and *Nonna* Maria, my aunt Argene and her two daughters, our family which consisted of five people including Aunt Nella from Lucca, and three neighbours from the adjoining house.

The next door neighbours were a very odd family indeed. They normally lived in *Fornaci*. In the spring of that year they had decided to move to the relative safety of our village. They ended up renting the adjoining house, which was vacant at the time.

The father of the family was called Amerigo. He was very thin and rather short and he had a very bad limp. He had been involved in an industrial accident while working in the munitions factory at *Fornaci*. He used a stick and when he walked he would suddenly jerk his right leg forward at every step.

His wife was called Ottavia. She was a big tall woman and she towered over her husband. Their son, who was called Alberto, was in his early twenties.

He was tall and somewhat fat with flabby skin. When he walked he had a tendency to flap his arms and I would not have been astonished if he had had webbed feet. He had in fact been rejected by the recruiting authorities as unsuitable for military service.

He had thick sensuous lips and he spoke in a falsetto voice. He was very effeminate and I found him very loathsome. He liked to boast of his numerous exploits and all his tales and jokes invariably had homosexual undertones. He was certainly not the type of person whose company I would willingly seek.

The Brazilians had been in Sommocolonia about a fortnight when they made their first attack on Lama. They were not very successful because the Germans were very deeply dug in and the road to Lama was uphill all the way. The weather was also very bad. They had chosen what had probably been one of the worst October days we had experienced: torrential rain most of the day with strong winds.

Added to this, the Brazilian troops wore American style boots with rubber soles and heels. This was the worst type of footwear for climbing up sodden muddy slopes. They slithered and slipped all over the place and suffered many casualties. We saw many wounded soldiers and several bodies brought back.

Towards the end of October, I was playing in the village square with some friends when a caravan of mules arrived with fresh supplies of food and ammunition The mule train stopped in the *piazza* and we boys hung around to watch the soldiers unload the mules. It was all very exciting to us. Besides, we were hoping to scrounge what we could from the soldiers.

Suddenly I heard the church bell strike four o'clock. I turned round and said to the others that I had to be off home for tea. Paolo Biondi asked me to hang on a little while longer. I would have loved to stay in the *piazza* to watch the soldiers finish unloading their supplies. I knew that if I did not go home soon I would be in trouble with Mother. So I set off and Benito and a few other boys followed me.

I had no sooner arrived home at *Monte*, than the Germans began to shell the village again. This time, some of the shells landed right in the *piazza* with terrible results: one mule was killed, two others were wounded and had to be put down. Among the human casualties three soldiers were wounded (one quite badly) and Paolo Biondi received several shrapnel wounds in various parts of the body.

Everyone thought that Paolo would not survive because he was really in a bad way. He was taken down to the hospital in Barga and shortly afterwards transferred to Lucca where he was operated on to remove various pieces of shrapnel.

After a lengthy period in hospital he eventually recovered. In fact, he lost one eye and did not manage to get back to Sommocolonia till much later in the year. He returned to the village just in time to experience the terrible events of the horrendous battle of 26th December.

I considered myself extremely lucky, for had I stayed behind that day for another ten minutes I might also have been a casualty with goodness knows what consequences.

A few days later, the Brazilian forces made another attempt at capturing Lama. This time they almost reached the German lines but they were repulsed again with very heavy casualties. The Germans had mined all the approaches to their lines and the Brazilian troops had to tread very warily over the last few yards thus becoming sitting ducks for the enemy machine gun posts.

That evening there were literally dozens and dozens of body bags lying in the square at the side of the church waiting to be taken away. This was their last attempt at an advance on Lama and, round about 5th November, the Brazilian forces were replaced by black American soldiers.

These American troops formed part of the segregated black US 92nd Infantry Division, known as the 'Buffalo soldiers'. At that time there was no integration in the US Army between blacks and whites. In fact the black Americans were treated as second class citizens by the upper echelons of the American military.

At first everyone was quite apprehensive at the arrival of all these black soldiers, for we still had not forgotten the scurrilous propaganda that had been disseminated by the Germans. Our apprehension was completely unfounded for we soon realised that we had nothing to fear from them. In fact they were extremely kind and generous towards the civilian population.

The Buffalo soldiers made their headquarters in *Nonno* Bonafede's house. It was quite a large house with five bedrooms, easily one of the largest in the village. Also, along with the *canonica*, it was one of only two houses in the village, which could boast a proper bathroom with running hot and cold water.

The plumbing was quite archaic however. The hot water was supplied by means of an ancient rather inefficient wood fired geyser. To light this boiler and get sufficient hot water for a bath was a whole day's operation and I don't think that Aunt Rosina and her family ever bothered with this strange contraption. They preferred to rely on the old fashioned method of heating pans of water.

Mother and Aunt Dora now started acting as interpreters between the American troops and the Italian partisans. They were paid in kind for their translation services. Among other things we received army blankets, army boots, various other items of military equipment, tinned food, emergency rations and literally thousands of American cigarettes. The four most popular brands of American cigarettes in order of popularity were Chesterfield, Lucky Strike, Camel and Raleigh.

We were also being constantly regaled with surplus food rations. One bedroom of our house was piled up with all kinds of goods. It was literally half full of these useful articles. Our luck was surely changing at last. We were no longer suffering the hardships of hunger as before. Furthermore, we had a large hoard of goods for bartering once the front line had passed.

We thought that we now possessed lots of bargaining power for everyday essentials and we would never go hungry again. If only we could have foretold the future and realised what was going to happen at Christmastime.

The Americans were particularly generous towards children and I would often be given chocolate and candies. I certainly took advantage of every opportunity that might present itself. On one occasion however, whilst fraternising with the soldiers, I got quite a shock.

At the side of the church there was a lean-to section, which served as a secondary entrance. The men of the village would always use this entrance and go and sit by themselves at one side of the church.

This kind of lobby lay in the lee of the medieval tower and was therefore quite sheltered from enemy bombardment. The American troops had decided to use this lobby way as an ammunition store. There were always two soldiers on guard duty in the doorway of this lean-to building. I would often go and chat to the sentries there in the hope of cadging some chocolate or the odd cigarette.

One day, while I was chatting away to the soldiers guarding all this ammunition, the Germans started one of their shelling bouts on the village. I looked around me. Suddenly I went cold all over with fear when I spotted the enormous amount of ammunition piled high nearby.

There was only a sloping roof without any loft and it was at this point that I realised the danger of being in this part of the church. There was nothing to stop a shell coming straight through the roof and exploding amidst the ammunition. It would certainly have made quite a pyrotechnic display! Anyone caught up in such an explosion would have had no chance of survival.

During the whole period of that bombardment I was inwardly trembling and I was convinced that this was going to be my last day alive. I was glad to leave after the shelling stopped. From that day I never again went to linger and chat to the sentries on duty at this particular post. I would just quickly greet the soldiers as I hurried past.

With the American HQ being in *Nonno* Bonafede's house, the place was a constant hive of activity. There were always visitors on some kind of official business. Often we would get people arriving in civilian clothes and we could only guess who they were or what their mission was.

One particular evening, shortly before Christmas, an Italian chap arrived, dressed in civvies. He chatted all evening, boasting of his various exploits as a spy. He said that he was going to go behind the enemy lines that night. He intimated that he was going to gather intelligence information about the Germans, their positions, their strength and their defences.

He left just before midnight and that was the last that anyone ever saw of him. Had he been captured by the Germans or was he perhaps a double agent?

There was a rumour going round that the allies were planning another assault on *Lama* around Christmastime. Was this going to be the 'big push' at last? Apparently it was called off at the last moment.

The village had certainly seen an influx of extra troops. They only stayed two or three days and they were suddenly pulled back two days before Christmas. The American Command had had a change of mind. Perhaps they wanted to celebrate a 'peaceful' Yuletide.

The defence of Sommocolonia was consequently left in the hands of two platoons of black American GIs and about twenty-five Italian partisans. They had obviously thought that these troops would be sufficient to hold this forward position until a possible intended advance sometime early in the New Year.

Chapter 15

Christmas Day 1944 was certainly cause for great joy. The Americans were truly celebrating in great style: roast turkey dinner with all the trimmings followed by ice cream for dessert. What a fantastic treat considering they were right in the front line.

Many of us thought that the Americans had very strange tastes, seeing that they were having jam along with their meat course. What we did not know at the time was that, this jam was cranberry sauce, the traditional American accompaniment to roast turkey.

The soldiers invited everyone to participate in their feast and so we all had a great meal, along with the troops. It was undoubtedly the best Christmas we had experienced for some years. However we were soon to pay dearly for all this unexpected bounty.

We had now been in the front line for nearly three months and the monotonous pattern of daily sporadic shelling had lulled everyone into a false sense of security. But the enemy troops had an altogether different fate in store for us. Had they perhaps been informed of the few soldiers remaining in Sommocolonia by the Italian spy of a few days earlier?

We went to bed quite happy that Christmas night. Life in the front line didn't seem so bad after all. True we had to contend with the dangers of the daily shelling. So far everyone except Mother and Paolo Biondi had managed to come through three months of this perilous life completely unscathed. Besides, we all felt that the allies would soon be making their decisive attack on the German lines. Once the Gothic Line had been overrun we could resume a normal life of peace and tranquillity again.

Shortly after midnight, there began a continuous artillery bombardment of the village, which lasted for over four hours. The shelling was almost non-stop and we were all absolutely terrified. For greater safety we decided to crawl under the beds but none of us managed to get any sleep that night.

Suddenly the shelling stopped and the battle for Sommocolonia began in earnest. Round about dawn the Axis Forces attacked the village coming in from the north. The Germans were advancing from house to house and we could now hear continual bursts of machine gun fire, sten and rifle shots.

Every now and then we would hear the sound of a bullet ricocheting off the bells in the campanile or the pitiful cry of a soldier who had fallen either dead or wounded.

At about nine o'clock that morning there was a lull in the fighting and all we could hear was the odd rifle shot. Mother decided to go upstairs into the Command Headquarters to look for some food for breakfast and, of course, she dragged me along with her.

When we got into the main living room we immediately saw a scene of unbelievable destruction. The entrance doorway at the front had been badly damaged and the glass-dividing wall inside was completely smashed. There was glass and debris everywhere.

All I wanted to do was go back into the relative safety of the cellar. Mother, on the other hand, pushed on into the large dining room next door as she had heard someone groaning. She looked around and, she saw the partisan commander, Lieutenant Sommati, lying there wounded on a settee. She knew him quite well because she was in daily contact with him in her role as interpreter.

In between his unintelligible groans Lieutenant Sommati managed to convey that he wanted a drink of water. Mother went to get him a cup of water and when she returned from the kitchen, she realised how badly wounded he was: the lower part of his face was extensively damaged. There was no recognisable mouth and Mother thought: 'where am I going to put the water?' While she was lifting his head to try and give him some water, he died in her arms.

After that, we didn't hang around to ask any questions. We quickly gathered together some bread and some biscuits and a container of water to take down into the basement for breakfast.

Back in the basement everyone crowded round us wanting to know what was happening. We didn't really have any idea on that score. We told them all about the extensive damage upstairs and how the partisan leader, Lieutenant Sommati, had died in Mother's arms

By about eleven o'clock in the morning, everyone was wondering what was happening. All seemed quiet on the battlefront and Mother decided to go upstairs again to try and get some information. This time she went on her own.

One of the officers informed her that the Allied Forces in the village had been completely overrun by overwhelming numbers of the enemy. The situation was untenable and it looked as though the only course of action would be to surrender to the Germans. They were not particularly looking forward to this. They knew only too well from past experience how their racist enemies would deal with black prisoners.

The American High Command further behind the lines had given the order for all the allied soldiers in Sommocolonia to abandon the village and retreat. At approximately midday they planned to send in aircraft to drop smoke bombs to mask their withdrawal. They assured them that with the help of this smoke screen they should easily be able to make it back to safety.

At twelve-thirty pm, another communication was received from Command Headquarters stating that the military would not be able to drop smoke bombs because there was too much wind that day. The final message was: "You are all to get the hell out of there and save your butts as best possible."

At about two pm, the few soldiers who were still alive began to file downstairs into the basement. They were going to leave by the basement door which led out into a section of the street that was less exposed.

They had with them two wounded soldiers. One was a private who had a very serious wound to one of his legs: His leg had been badly shattered and he could only walk using his rifle as a crutch.

A lengthy discussion took place. The seriously wounded soldier was in no position to make a hasty retreat. The most sensible solution would be to leave him behind. At this the soldier begged them to take him along with them because he did not want to end up as a 'doomed' prisoner.

A decision had to be made quickly. Then an officer declared that he would be left behind. In order to help him, a sergeant, who had a minor wound to his forehead, opted to remain behind in the basement and keep the crippled soldier company. The remainder of the troops then said goodbye and quickly filed out of the basement through the side door.

There now began a period of ominous silence, which proved to be even more terrifying than the infernal noise of the artillery bombardment during the previous night. Did this unnatural silence presage some new impending disaster?

We remained in the basement for an hour or so, dreadfully waiting with baited breath for the enemy soldiers to enter the building. What would happen if the Germans were to find us together with two black American GIs? Fortunately we didn't find out.

At around three-thirty pm, Mother and Aunt Dora ventured out to find out what was happening. Less than five minutes later they came back out of breath. They had gone as far as the priest's house where they had been told that the Germans had given orders that all civilians must evacuate the village because they were going to set fire to all the buildings.

It was now imperative that we leave. We didn't know where we were going to end up that night but one thing was certain: we couldn't remain in the basement. We would undoubtedly need some form of bedding. And so we began to gather together everything we could find. The easiest way to carry all this bedding was to drape the sheets and blankets over our shoulders.

The two wounded American soldiers wanted to come with us. Everyone said that we could not take them along with us as it was too dangerous. The two soldiers kept beseeching us not to leave them behind.

After a lot of discussion and speculation, Mother and Aunt Dora overruled everyone else and, the two American soldiers followed us, with bedding draped over their heads and shoulders. This way they looked just like civilians.

As we made our way towards the priest's house we came across dead soldiers lying in the road. When we arrived at the *canonica* we found that the house was empty. They had obviously taken heed of the Germans' threat and left very quickly.

We continued to wend our way through the streets taking care not to stumble over the dead bodies strewn almost everywhere. When we eventually reached the house of Armido Marchetti at the southern edge of the village, we could hear that there were people inside and we decided to join them.

It took quite some time for us all to file into the building. I was the last person to enter. All the while I kept looking around to see if I could see any sign of the Germans. Then, as I was looking along the fields skirting the house, I perceived what looked like a German machine gun emplacement in the distance.

In my youthful naivety I started to point in that direction in amazement. Then, as I was just about to enter the house, the Germans suddenly strafed the building with machine gun fire. Fortunately, the bullets hit the wall just above my head. Nevertheless I didn't hang around to find out whether they were just warning shots. My only thoughts were for my safety.

Terrified I dived into the building with lightning speed. When we arrived down into the basement we found quite a crowd there. In fact it seemed as though half the village was huddled in that confined space. There were easily thirty people or more in the basement. With the addition of our little band numbering over twenty in all, it got quite crowded in that rather small area.

Chapter 16

During the terrifying non-stop bombardment by the Germans, Armido's family and the Olivieri family who lived next door had made a hole in the dividing wall between the two basements so as to provide a means of communication between them. The hole was barely wide enough for a person to crawl through but in this way, the two families had been able to keep up each other's spirits during that previous dreadful night.

We had been in the basement of Armido's house for only about five minutes when we learnt that the Germans had established their command Headquarters in the Olivieri house next door.

When we heard this we were rather taken aback because here we were with the two wounded American soldiers that we had helped to save. Everyone was saying "Get rid of those Americans otherwise we will all be shot". Mother and Dora would have none of it declaring: "We are not going to abandon them. They're human beings just like us."

Then suddenly a German soldier crawled through the hole between the two houses and began to search the basement. Fortunately we had hidden the American soldiers under the beds.

The basement was very dimly lit by a couple of oil lamps. In the semi darkness the soldier only gave everyone a cursory glance in his task of ascertaining that we were all civilians. He had also been somewhat hampered in his search by the fact that there were so many of us all huddled together in that small space.

When the sentry left, Mother and Dora decided that it would perhaps be wiser to hide the wounded soldiers elsewhere. It was now getting dark and they took the two GIs upstairs out of the front door. Outside, across a small yard, was a stable. Mother and Dora led the soldiers into this stable and advised them to bury themselves deeply in the straw. They left them there saying that they would try and call back the following morning to see how they were doing.

No sooner had they got back to the basement than two German soldiers arrived and made a more thorough search. This time they meticulously looked everywhere even under the beds. When they were satisfied with the results of their perusal they returned to their headquarters next door.

We felt very relieved and considered ourselves extremely lucky. Had the Germans found the two American soldiers we would all have been shot. We had our suspicions that someone in the house next door had informed the Germans that we had some American soldiers with us. We were 99% certain that a particular person had been responsible for this. This fellow had a reputation for being an opportunist. We could not prove it but what other feasible explanation could there be for what had just happened?

Whilst Mother and Dora were quietly discussing this matter among themselves, one of the sentries came back into our section of the basement and remained on guard there all night.

Later that evening Barga was being bombarded by the Germans with artillery fire. From a narrow opening on the southern edge of the basement we could see Barga being hit. In the blackness of the night it looked as if the whole town was ablaze. The German sentry kept saying to us in broken Italian with obvious delight: "*Guardare bella Barga. Bruciare bene.*" Look beautiful Barga. It burn well. (Foreign troops found Italian verb tenses very complicated and difficult. They overcame this problem by using the infinitive of the verb and modifying it with an adverb or adverbial phrase of time.)

We were now quite apprehensive about the future. What other misfortunes would befall us the next day? In the cramped quarters of that small basement area we could barely find sufficient room to sit down. Despite the discomfort we did manage to snatch some sleep because we were absolutely exhausted after the ordeal of the previous night.

The next morning the Germans ordered all the civilians to evacuate the village and declared that they would shoot anyone who had not left by midday. Mother, showing incredible courage, went next door and walked up into the German Headquarters. She held Aldo in her arms and dragged me along by the hand.

Inside the house there were German soldiers everywhere. Most of them were sitting on the floor around a long room, smoking and talking. They all looked at us in amazement.

Mother shouted out loud that she had two children to feed and shelter and needed someone to accompany her to her house. They all started to jeer and make fun of her. Mother however kept insisting that she needed food for her two children. Finally one of the soldiers took pity on her and offered to accompany her.

We set off to go back up to Wanda's house. On the way, we noticed in one of the side roads the blackened bodies of three American soldiers. The Germans had torched a house when they found out that it contained black American troops. In flames, the soldiers had jumped out of the ground floor windows trying to escape the inferno. The Germans had shown no mercy towards them and had deliberately gunned them down.

We walked very warily up to the house. We were worried that some German soldier might decide to take a pot shot at us. After what seemed like an eternity we arrived there. We found that the house had been damaged during the battle and we were only able to reach a few odds and ends. We quickly gathered up some food and hurried back to Armido's house.

Whilst we were away the Germans had issued another stern ultimatum. On arriving there we found that everyone was getting ready to leave the basement. No one doubted that the Germans were serious, and so, mid-morning we all set off to flee from the village, taking with us whatever we could.

I was carrying Aldo on my shoulders so that I had my hands free to carry two bags. Mother also carried as much as she could on her shoulders. We had tied our bedding into bundles so as to make them easier to carry.

Everyone was hesitating and wondering which way to go when suddenly the Germans helped us on our way by letting off a few bursts of machine gun fire in our direction. No one was hit because the bullets went flying well above our heads. It nevertheless certainly convinced us that they were not bluffing. The fear of being hit spurred us on and we started running down the mountain to get as far away as possible from the village.

We eventually arrived at *Pruno*, the summer hut belonging to the Passerotti family. This hut was literally crammed with people who, like us, had run away from the village. Inside, several old ladies, all dressed in black, were wailing and weeping. Some were shouting: "*Gesummaria. Che cosa faremo?*" (Sweet Jesus and Mary. What are we going to do?) Others kept reciting the rosary.

It was quite a bright clear winter's day and I decided to go and lie on my back in one of the fields away from all the woe. How lovely it was to sit outside and enjoy the peaceful silence. The silence was suddenly shattered by the monotonous drone of aircraft. Then I saw them coming over the horizon.

I watched them with great interest wondering what they were going to do. Then I noticed what looked like little balloons floating from them. My first thought was: "How strange. I wonder why they are dropping balloons?" It didn't take me long to realise that they were not balloons but bombs. I was suddenly overcome with fear because it really looked as though the bombs were going to land right on top of us.

I jumped up and went running into the hut and shouted that we had to run away because they were dropping bombs. One of the old women in black said: "*Dina, di' a quel tuo figliolo matto di star zitto.*" (Dina, why don't you tell that stupid son of yours to be quiet.) A few seconds later the bombs fell on Sommocolonia with the devastating sound of explosions. At the same time the hut shook to its very foundations. I thought to myself: "Who's the stupid son now?"

The bombing had an electrifying effect on everybody. Without hesitation everyone picked up their few belongings and ran off again to seek shelter and safety elsewhere. We then headed towards the bottom of the mountain.

As we were running away, even more aircraft came over the horizon to bomb and machine gun the village. We were quite safe from the bombing, but the empty shells of the heavy calibre machine gun bullets kept falling through the trees all around us.

We reckoned that these empty cartridge shells would probably not kill us. We were nevertheless still quite frightened because they were rather large and we could easily sustain a nasty wound should one of them land on our heads.

That first night we stopped at the *Mulino dei Gasperetti* (The Gasperetti water mill) at the side of the torrent *Corsonna*. This was the very mill that supplied the village with electricity. We spent one night in the adjoining stable before we moved on.

This time we went to stay at a place called *Le Paradise* only two or three hundred yards from Catagnana. *Le Paradise* consisted of two houses, which were right close to the *mulattiera*. Under better circumstances it would most probably have been a heavenly and idyllic place for a peaceful sojourn. At that moment it just meant somewhere for us to stay.

I do not know why we came to end up at *Le Paradise*. I gathered some time later that the houses belonged to a family who had emigrated to England. They normally used these houses as holiday homes for their enlarged family whenever they came back to Italy on holiday. I can only assume that they belonged to someone who was distantly related to us.

In the house next door to us, an old widow (well she seemed an old lady to me at the time) had taken shelter with her two daughters Amabile and Irma. Amabile was a pretty girl of twenty-two and her sister Irma was four years younger. They normally lived on top of the *Montatella* (little slope) in Sommocolonia. I never discovered the mother's Christian name. Her surname was Togneri and she was known to everyone as *La Tognera*.

I had received my Epiphany present early that year. It was a brand new pair of shoes, which I needed very badly. I was very proud of those shoes. Unfortunately Aunt Dora had commandeered them. She reckoned she needed them to help her run away quickly. I consequently was reduced to wearing my old pair of shoes, which had holes in the soles. Dora, despite her chubbiness, was certainly able to run nearly as fast as I did. It was almost as though she was wearing magic shoes!

Watching Aunt Nella sprinting to keep up with everyone was quite astounding. She had recently sprained an ankle very badly and had only been able to walk with great difficulty. In fact she had spent the whole of the last two days, prior to Christmas, in the basement, insisting that she could not use her leg. It was amazing to see how the exigencies of escaping from danger had 'miraculously' cured her bad ankle!

Aunt Dora and Nella only stayed one night. Nella wanted to get back home to Lucca. Dora agreed to go along with her. She also took with her a friend from Barga called Quinta. Quinta was either a widow or an unmarried mother and she had a daughter called Anna who was about my age.

Chapter 17

One of the partisans defending the village was of Yugoslav origin. He absolutely hated the Nazis because they had killed his whole family. He swore to have his revenge and he joined the partisan movement.

He was a fluent German speaker and was able to lull individual German soldiers into a false sense of security. When he had lured them to somewhere sheltered he would cold-bloodedly cut their throats. He reckoned he had killed dozens during his time as a partisan. It was rumoured that during the battle of Sommocolonia he managed to kill about ten of the enemy in this manner before he himself became a casualty.

The people of Sommocolonia had been very lucky. Out of a population of well over 200 people only two had been wounded up till then: mother by the Brazilians at the beginning of the front line and Paolo Biondi a few weeks later when the Germans had shelled the village square.

However the events of 26th/27th December 1944 were to prove quite different. During those two days there would be several casualties, both dead and wounded, among the civilian population.

The first person to be killed was a man called Mario Cassettari. He had been a soldier in the Italian army serving on the Greek front. One night while he was sitting with a group of fellow soldiers around a campfire behind the lines a cannon shell landed right in the middle of the group.

Fortunately it did not explode. Nevertheless, this had a terrifying effect on Mario. He became shell-shocked and he eventually had to be given a discharge from the Italian army on medical grounds.

When he returned to Sommocolonia everyone remarked that he was a completely different person and from being a normal cheerful chap he had developed an altogether different personality. During the front line he was constantly afraid of being shot. Was this perhaps a premonition of the fate that was to befall him?

Mario's family lived right on the northeastern edge of the village. When the front line arrived, Mario would not live in this house, for, in his opinion, it was too dangerous.

The family decided to move to a basement under the *Rocca*. This was probably the safest basement in the village. There were four storeys above it and the doorway was in a very narrow alleyway, which was practically surrounded on all sides by tall buildings. Furthermore, it lay in the lee of the medieval tower. Cannon and mortar shells would never be able to penetrate this natural 'fortress'.

The family would go about their normal business during the daytime. Mario, on the other hand, declared that it was too dangerous to venture outside and he remained in that basement day and night. As time progressed, the family slowly convinced him that there was really no danger for during a period of well over three months nobody had been killed and only one person (Paolo Biondi) had been injured by the German shelling.

He was finally persuaded by his family to move back into their family home at the northeastern entrance to the village. They moved there just one week before Christmas. I believe that the family was really intending to move out of the front line area as soon as possible after Christmas.

The Cassettari basement lay in the lee of the mountain and it would have been impossible for a German shell to hit there. The basement was at street level and the door led straight onto the road. When the Germans entered the village from the north, the first door they came to, was that of the Cassettari household. They hammered on the door with their rifle butts. Mario went to open the heavy basement door. For no apparent reason, the Germans just shot him point blank without any warning.

Mario was killed instantly. His daughter reckoned that the German troops had possibly thought that he was a partisan. How incredibly strange! His haunting incubus had come true. His fear of being shot had actually materialised into fact.

The German soldiers then went on to the next two houses and strafed the doors with automatic fire. No one knows why they had decided to fire away in such an indiscriminate manner but the most plausible theory that was put forward was that the Germans had probably thought that these basements were full of partisans lying in wait.

This may have been because someone had shouted *paesan* (villager). The Germans had probably mistaken this word to be *partigian* (partisan). In the heat of battle the words *paesan* and *partigian* when uttered by a nervous person through a stout wooden door, could easily have been misunderstood.

The second door they came to was that of the Nardini household. Nardino, the eldest child who was my age and had taken his first communion on the same day as me, was wounded. His little baby brother who was being held in his mother's arms was killed outright, and his mother was shot in her arm.

Nardino received seven bullets in one leg. He was in a dreadful state and his family thought he was going to die. He was first taken to the hospital in Barga. There, all the medical personnel had run away. When the Germans retreated, Nardino was transferred to the main civilian hospital in Lucca.

This hospital in Lucca was full to overflowing: in fact they had to accommodate two children to a bed. After a few days Nardino was taken to a Military Field Hospital in Pisa. For the first three months all they did was medicate his wounds. Then he was transferred back and forth to and from the Lucca hospital.

After about nine months he was transferred back to Barga hospital where he had all the bullets removed except one. They had had to leave this last bullet 'in situ' because it would have been too dangerous to try and remove it. He ended up with a rigid leg and a crooked foot. When he returned to Sommocolonia in the spring of 1946, the engineering branch of the forces were busy exploding all the mines and dangerous ammunition that had been lying around in the various stores.

One day, when they suddenly caused a particularly loud explosion Nardino got a terrible fright because he thought that the wartime shelling had started again. The shock caused him to fall off the wall where he was sitting. He landed awkwardly on his crooked foot and broke it.

He was now taken back to the local hospital where they straightened his foot and set it in plaster. As a consequence of all these injuries he was left with no movement in his leg except at the hip. Nardino still has a rigid leg sixty years later.

The worst civilian casualties were the Cascianella family. They lived on the other side of the village near the spot where I had seen the German machine gun emplacement when we were escaping. The Americans had billeted a small squad of soldiers in their house. When the Germans surrounded the house they ordered everyone out. As they rushed out they were all gunned down, soldiers and civilians.

The only surviving member of the Cascianella family was a young boy of eleven who had run out first. The Germans let this boy pass unchallenged but when they saw the black American troops they just fired away indiscriminately. They showed no mercy whatsoever towards any of the black troops during the battle. And so, along with the soldiers, six members of the Cascianella family were killed: father, mother, who was seven months pregnant, and three children.

A few days later, when the village was recaptured by the allied troops they found the two black American GIs that Mother and Dora had hidden in the stable. They were ravenously hungry and had started to eat raw turnips but they had survived. The soldier with the badly damaged leg had to have it amputated but at least his life had been saved.

Mother and Aunt Dora were informed by the American military authorities that they would be given a medal by the American government for their brave efforts in saving these two soldiers. These promises came to nothing for even to this day nothing has transpired.

In fact it took over fifty years for the American authorities to even recognise and honour the courageous deeds of their own black soldiers.

Out of a company of 95 American soldiers and 25 Italian partisans stationed in Sommocolonia, only 18 (including the two we had managed to save) escaped with their lives.

The battle of Sommocolonia was a very tragic event indeed. Not only was it one of the bloodiest engagements of the whole Italian campaign, but it was also the only real battle fought on Tuscan soil during the Second World War.

Netto, the ex proprietor of the *Sali e tabacchi* shop was another victim of this battle. It was on 27th December when, despite being warned by his family not to do so, Netto, decided to go and feed his cow. The byre was situated just a few yards below the village and when the Germans spotted him they machine-gunned him down without hesitation. They may have thought that he was a partisan.

Everyone had his or her own tale to tell about that disastrous battle. The parish priest, Don Fredianelli, was forcefully recruited along with several other able bodied men to carry German casualties (wounded and dead) back behind their own lines.

They had thought that they would end up being transported back to Germany in the same manner as all the civilians caught up in the *rastrellamenti* prior to the front line. They were very lucky because after about 18 hours of almost incessant stretcher bearing the Germans suddenly decided to release them.

The War Memorial to the dead villagers of both World Wars clearly indicates the effect on the population of Sommocolonia. This War Memorial, which is situated just outside the main church of San Frediano, illustrates the difference between the two World Wars. In the First World War, all the victims were soldiers who perished fighting in the campaign on the Austrian front. In contrast the greater part of the victims of the Second World War were civilians who died during the battle of Sommocolonia.

An amusing story is told of three old people who were rather deaf. Two of them were Marino Vincenti's grandparents, called Andrea &

Lisa. The third person was a woman called Lisone, who lodged with them. She was a strange character for she always went around barefoot. All three of them were very fond of a tipple.

During the evening of 26th December, on finding all the wine cellars open, they went and helped themselves and had quite a party. The next day when everyone had to evacuate they were the only three people to remain behind. Apparently they were still drinking and were very merry indeed. When the Americans bombed the village, destroying houses all around them they were completely oblivious to the noise and destruction that was taking place.

They were eventually chased out of the village by the Indian troops. Days later when they were recounting their adventure, one of them said: "*Che sbornia che si era fatto! Tremavano anche le case!*" (What a 'skinful' we had! Why even the houses were shaking!) What bliss to be so happily inebriated as to be completely unaware of bombs dropping all round them!

Chapter 18

In 1973, an American couple from California, Solace (Sally) Wales Sheets and her husband Bill bought a holiday home in Sommocolonia. They had both fallen in love with the village and Bill, who was an artist, considered this to be an ideal place for pursuing his talents as a painter. In fact he turned the top floor of his house into an artist's studio.

I have known Sally and Bill Sheets for several years by meeting them every summer when I go over to spend a quiet vacation in my house, formerly belonging to *Nonno* Bonafede. Over the years they have become good friends of both my family and myself.

One day when Sally was exploring Sommocolonia, she came across a monument to the Italian partisans who had fallen whilst trying to defend the village from the advancing Germans on 26th December 1944. This monument is situated on a hillock immediately above the car park at the northernmost edge of the village.

Sally noticed, that among the several stone markers commemorating the deaths of the Italian partisans, there was one marker which read: "John Fox, U.S. Army Lieutenant, December 26th 1944." This aroused Sally's curiosity and she began to ask her Italian neighbours about this John Fox. Little by little she pieced together the story of the battle, the role of the Buffalo soldiers and the partisans. It was then that she learnt that John Fox was one of the American GIs who had died during the battle of Sommocolonia.

Sally now began to wonder what had really happened on that day in December 1944. What was John Fox's role in the battle and why was there no monument to him and his comrades?

The brave story of John Fox is briefly as follows. He was a black Lieutenant in the American Army. He was in fact an artillery spotter.

His post was in the medieval tower on the *Rocca* and his role was that of directing allied artillery against the enemy by pinpointing coordinates for the American gunners.

Early on the morning of 26th December, when he was awakened by the incessant shelling of the village by the German Army, John Fox rushed to his battle post on the tower.

When the Axis Forces broke through the allied defences on the northern edge of the village, John Fox suddenly became aware of the fact that the road below the *Rocca* was full of the advancing enemy.

The Germans had in fact sent in elements of Austrian infantry who formed part of the elite Fourth Mountain Battalion. These were highly trained troops specialising in mountain warfare.

The Axis Forces had chosen a most appropriate moment for the attack. The soldiers of the 92nd Infantry Division stationed in Sommocolonia were no match for the overwhelming numbers of enemy troops that were thrown against them.

Not only were there very few defenders, but they were also very poorly equipped to deal with the masses of crack troops that they were facing. Furthermore the attack came as a complete surprise. Instead of celebrating Christmas Day the Germans had been secretly taking up their positions for their offensive at dawn the following morning.

When John Fox saw the advancing enemy below he radioed in a set of coordinates, which would result in the shells hitting the area of the *Rocca*. His friend and fellow officer Otis Zachary was on the other end of the line. Otis Zachary knew exactly what these latest coordinates meant.

At first he refused to do what his friend had asked him. He and John Fox had known each other for some time. They had trained together as officer cadets in the same unit in the United States and had even sailed over to the European theatre on the same boat. No way was he going to kill a good friend in this manner. John Fox kept insisting and Otis Zachary kept refusing.

Eventually Otis, against his better judgement, was forced to turn his guns on his old pal after being ordered to do so by a superior officer.

Many years later, Otis recounted that he had been plagued for years by this decision and still had nightmares decades later.

Don Fredianelli, the villages priest, who had been 'commandeered' by the Germans for stretcher duty, remembered seeing the body of John Fox on the *Rocca* surrounded by the corpses of several of the enemy.

When Sally went back home to California she started making extensive enquiries. At first she did not know whether there had been any survivors among the fellow Americans who had been defending the village.

One of the first things she found out was that John Fox's widow, Arlene and their daughter Sandra, along with several other widows and relatives of veteran Buffalo soldiers, had been pestering the Pentagon for many years. They wanted the brave deeds of these soldiers to be recognised.

With typical bureaucratic pigheadedness the authorities refused to budge on this matter. These heroes were black and in the Pentagon's eyes they could be forgotten. They declared that that chapter in the war was now history. The books had been closed and no further honours could be bestowed. Only an Act of Congress could change matters.

Sally then contacted Arlene Fox and other widows of the veterans of that campaign. Through sheer persistent determination they managed to get Congress to change their minds and on 13th January 1997, John Fox was posthumously awarded the Congressional Medal of Honour, along with six other black Americans for their actions during the Second World War.

Sally's efforts did not end here. She campaigned for a reunion to be held in Italy so that the courageous GIs could be honoured in the region where they had fought. And so a reunion was organised for Sunday 16th July 2000.

I myself ensured that I would sojourn to my holiday home early that year so as to be present at the celebrations. Sommocolonia had become famous for a day. The village was buzzing with representatives of the world's media. There were several newspaper correspondents, American, English and Italian, including 'The Times' of London.

There were also two television companies whose apparent intention was to make a film of the events. Some of the villagers were interviewed by the world's press and I personally was filmed and interviewed by several reporters.

That weekend I met John Fox's widow Arlene, their daughter Sandra and several veterans of the Buffalo soldiers. I entertained all these Americans in my house, which is adjacent to the tower where John Fox bravely died. I explained to them that the house had been the headquarters of the Buffalo soldiers stationed in Sommocolonia. It would be here that John Fox would have been billeted when not on observation duty.

Among the veterans were Otis Zachary, the gunnery officer and two actual survivors of the battle of Sommocolonia. I accompanied one of them around the village and together we identified the house where he had been at his post, manning a heavy calibre machine gun, on the morning of the battle.

Otis Zachary remembered very well the racial discrimination in the American Forces at the time. His very words on the day of the reunion were: "In those days if you were not white, you had to fight on two fronts. One against the Nazis and another against the mentality of your own superiors." There were a few other veteran survivors of the battle who would have loved to have been present. Unfortunately, they were too frail to undertake the long journey from America.

The reunion happened to coincide with the triennial celebrations for Our Lady of Mount Carmel. There were many dignitaries present: the American Consul from Florence, the mayor of Barga, several Buffalo veterans, representatives of the Italian Alpini and various civic leaders.

The day really belonged to Arlene Fox, John Fox's widow, her family and the GI veterans of the campaign. In the morning they were officially welcomed by the mayor of Barga in the municipal chambers. There followed a solemn mass in the church of *San Frediano* in Sommocolonia, which was celebrated by Don Piero, the then provost of the Barga region.

Later in the morning there was an official ceremony dedicated to *La Pace* (Peace) on the *Rocca*. There followed the inevitable speeches.

Nevertheless it was a very poignant occasion and many people had tears in their eyes.

The official party together with their American guests then proceeded to the international Hotel *Il Ciocco* at Castelvecchio Pascoli for a meal. In the late afternoon Arlene Fox returned to Sommocolonia to open an exhibition of photographs held in the small church of *San Rocco* in the village square.

Those black GIs, who had so courageously fought and perished in the battle of Sommocolonia, had finally been truly honoured by both Governments. What a wonderful start to the Third Millennium!

A few of the headlines of the International Press recalling this momentous occasion:

American

New York Times:

On a 1944 Battleground. Salute for a Black Hero

San Francisco Chronicle:

Italian Town honours black GIs who were shunned by their own country.

Herald Tribune:

Remembering the Fallen in the World's War

The Cincinnati Enquirer:

Veteran celebrated in Italy. Lt. John Fox received Medal of Honour for defending village

Newsweek:

As Good as Anybody Else. Their white officers called them cowards, but a hill town in Tuscany honours the Buffalo Soldiers' heroism in WW II

English

The Times:

GI haunted by hero friend he had to kill.

Italian

La Nazione:

Torna a Sommocolonia lo spirito eroico del tenente americano Fox

Il Tirreno:

Dagli USA a Sommocolonia per ricordare il sacrificio di militari, civili e partigiani

Il Giornale di Barga:

Le celebrazioni di Sommocolonia

L'ora di Barga:

Una giornata indimenticabile a Sommocolonia

Chapter 19

At the time we had all been extremely annoyed when the German troops insisted that we had to evacuate the village on the morning of 27th December 1944. Sommocolonia was our home after all and the Brazilian and American soldiers had allowed us to stay. Could the Germans not have been more understanding towards us? However, their harsh actions turned out to be a blessing in disguise. Had we still been in the village later that day when the Americans started dropping bombs, there is no doubt that many more civilians would have been killed.

The American bombing of the village caused an enormous amount of damage. Over half the houses were destroyed or extensively damaged and hardly a building remained unscathed during that unforgettable afternoon of the 27th December 1944. The tower, which had been standing for hundreds of years, received a direct hit.

During the German artillery bombardments, cannon shells just bounced off the ultra thick walls of the tower but the American bomb which had scored a direct hit destroyed one whole side and left it in ruins. The American authorities had stated that they would rebuild this tower as part of the war damage reparation programme but, like many of their other promises, this came to nothing.

Immediately after the war there was a lot of talk about restoring the tower to its former glory. A local *Geometra* (surveyor) even went as far as drawing up plans for rebuilding the tower.

These plans came to nothing because the local *Comune* could not afford the expense involved and the American authorities had reneged on their promise to provide funds as part of their war reparations. And so the tower just continued to deteriorate until it reached the present state of disrepair. The latest plan is that the C*omune* is to embark on a limited operation to render the ruins safe.

Only about half of the badly damaged buildings were eventually rebuilt after the frontline. In actual fact, although no one realised it at the time, this irreparable damage was to mark a turning point in the history of the village. From being a thriving community it gradually began to decline.

In the early 1960's the life of the village received a terrific boost when the authorities constructed a new asphalted road for motor vehicles. They did not follow the track of the old roman road (*mulattiera*) but built a brand new *strada carrozzabile* which snaked back and forth in a very gradual gradient. This road led to a purpose built car park at the edge of the village just before reaching the *piazza San Rocco*.

A further short branch of the road was also constructed which led to the northernmost edge of the village where a second car park was built. This car park leads to the *Piazza dei Martiri* where the monument to the fallen partisans was erected.

Now that the village could be reached by car, an enterprising villager, Paolo Biondi, the same chap who had lost an eye during the German shelling of the *piazza* in October 1944, built a restaurant with rooms just at the end of the car park. Paolo's cooking was typical of the cuisine of that area: true regional gastronomy without pretentiousness, at a price affordable by everyone. Paolo soon built up quite a reputation for quality and value.

Most of his trade was at weekends when people would flock to the restaurant from miles around. On weekdays he was not so busy with his restaurant but his bar was always crowded with villagers. There were now two bars in the village. Whereas it was previously showing signs of serious decline it was now experiencing a real 'social renascence'.

Unfortunately this did not last very long. The oil crisis of 1973 had a devastating effect on Paolo's business. Italy at that time was totally dependent on imported petroleum products for most of its energy requirements. In order to conserve fuel the Italian Government issued an order that all non-essential vehicular traffic was prohibited at weekends. As Paolo relied on motorists driving up to Sommocolonia at weekends, his business suffered a drastic downturn. And so it was not long before he decided to close his restaurant and bar business altogether.

The village now started really going downhill. The younger inhabitants preferred the livelier life of the town and many of them had decided to leave Sommocolonia and go and live in nearby towns. As the older inhabitants began to die off they were not replaced by new blood, and so the population of the village started to decrease very considerably.

The beautiful church of *San Frediano* had also received a direct hit by a bomb and had been completely reduced to rubble. Almost miraculously, the campanile, which was situated next to the church, was left standing, although for a long time afterwards it was considered unsafe. Despite all the apparent damage, the campanile is now in full use again after very little restoration.

Another strange thing was that the War Memorial which stands right next to the campanile, also came through all the shelling and bombing unscathed. The church itself was rebuilt after the war to the exact same plan as the one that was destroyed.

Wanda's house, which was situated next to the church, had been extensively damaged and consequently we were unable to salvage any of the goods, which we had stored in the upstairs room. We had, like most other families in Sommocolonia, lost everything.

The German advance on Sommocolonia was part of a greater campaign to try and reach the main allied supply depot just south of Lucca. These stores were all amassed alongside the *autostrada Firenze-Mare*, the stretch between Lucca and the coast. As far as the eye could see, all kinds of equipment were stacked in the open air: jeeps, lorries, numerous types of vehicles and all kinds of ordnance.

And there were makeshift buildings scattered all along the route. These also housed all manner of military materiel.

The Germans were desperate for supplies and it was really fortunate that their advance did not reach that far. Another one of their goals was the port of Livorno. Had they been able to capture this important port they could have cut the allied main supply route. This would have undoubtedly extended their stay in the Gothic Line

When the Americans started to bomb the areas newly occupied by the enemy, the Germans soon abandoned their plans and retreated back to their former positions.

On 28th/29th December the allies brought in the Eighth Indian Infantry Division to drive the Germans back. They were Sikhs who wore turbans and they were commanded by British officers. The latest German propaganda rumour was that these Indians would rape all the women and everyone was terrified. Again this proved unfounded for they were very disciplined troops.

It was really wonderful to watch these Sikh soldiers make their way up the mountain in battle formation. They advanced slowly but effectively, covering each other all the time. As it turned out they did not get involved in a battle with the enemy because the Germans had already abandoned the village.

Meanwhile we found ourselves worse off than before the arrival of the front line. We had practically nil possessions and little food. Mother was no longer acting as interpreter and we could not rely on these perks any more

Two days later Mother announced that we were going up to Sommocolonia to try and salvage and retrieve some of our property. So off we went, Mother and I. When we reached the last bit of slope just before entering the village we were challenged to stop by an armed sentry. Mother just kept on going, waving all the time and shouting: "It's alright, we're English".

The sentry completely ignored Mother's entreaties, and when we got closer he stopped us at bayonet point. He certainly made it crystal clear that he was deadly serious. He then shepherded us, still at bayonet point, to their Headquarters.

The Sikh soldiers had set up their headquarters in the Olivieri house. This was probably because it was one of the very few houses, which had not been damaged. Inside the Headquarters Mother was interrogated for quite a considerable period of time by a British officer.

He wanted to know what we were doing trying to enter the front line positions. When Mother tried to explain that she was only interested in gathering together any food and other commodities for her starving children he wasn't concerned in the least.

Finally he said to Mother: "Madam you must consider yourself a very lucky woman. This village is in a restricted area and is therefore out of bounds to all civilians. My men have orders to shoot anyone who disregards their commands to stop. If ever you come back again I shall not be responsible for your safety." We quickly left empty-handed. In fact we never tried to go back to the village again until after the front line had passed.

Within a few days the Indian troops were replaced by a fresh batch of Buffalo soldiers. Amabile, who lived in the house next to us, had always been a bit of a flirt and we soon realised that she and her sister were quite a magnet for soldiers who were looking for female company.

La Tognera did not mind because the soldiers were very generous and generally harmless. But one night we were called to their house because there were two American soldiers who were quite drunk. As sometimes happens when people get drunk, one of the soldiers was proving to be quite objectionable. La Tognera expected Mother to talk to them in English and get rid of them.

In cases like these one has to be rather diplomatic with drunks and humour them along to a certain extent. But La Tognera got quite annoyed at the fact that these soldiers were showing no signs of leaving and angrily said: "*Quando vanno via questi neracci?*" (When are these dirty niggers leaving?) The soldier who was being very objectionable apparently understood a fair amount of Italian. When he heard what La Tognera had said he literally went berserk and started shooting.

Fortunately, the bullets harmlessly hit the ceiling but we were all scared out of our wits. Mother then tried to calm him and with the help of his fellow soldier managed to get him out of the door. Then she immediately locked the door behind them. The drunken soldier just stood outside and kept shouting that if we did not open the door he would shoot the 'Goddam' lock off. All this time his colleague kept trying to restrain him.

Mother and La Tognera then decided that someone had to go and seek help. So I was delegated as being the most agile. This meant that I had to go upstairs and climb out of the back bedroom window. They lowered me down from the window and I jumped the last few feet. Then I ran like the wind to Catagnana to the command Headquarters to seek help.

Some of the men on guard came back with me and arrested the drunken soldier and led him back to their camp. That was the end of that incident for I do not think those two soldiers ever came back to the house.

We were still struggling to find enough food. The next day we heard that one of the mules taking supplies up to the village had slipped and broken a leg. Consequently it had to be put down.

The best part of this accident was that the soldiers had decided that it would be a shame to waste this meat and they proceeded to distribute it to the civilians. Mother made sure that we would get some of this unexpected bounty. She managed to get a few mule steaks. The meat was quite tough but I nevertheless declared it to be quite tasty. In consequence of this I can truthfully say: "One should always savour a gift mule in the mouth!"

Mother now resumed her attempts to get us repatriated to the UK. A British colonel in Barga had told her that he would definitely get her back to England. The following day we duly presented ourselves to the appointed place just over the footbridge in Barga.

The colonel had indeed laid on a military utility vehicle to take us off to Lucca. We got in the vehicle and no sooner had we set off than a German shell hit the very spot where our vehicle had been standing just a second or two before. We were terrified and at the same time we were happy because we thought that we would soon be out of the battle zone and on our way to England.

In Lucca, we were taken to a refugee camp. It was an enormous building, which had obviously been some kind of institution. Inside, it was anything but welcoming: there were enormous open plan areas and we were billeted in a section, which was shut off with metal bars. This made it seem very much like a prison. Although it was financed by the allies, it was run by the Italian authorities.

The food was absolutely disgusting and completely inedible. They insisted on making my brother Aldo drink a horrible liquid which they had concocted by reconstituting poor quality milk powder. It may have been all right for cooking but as a drink it was indescribably awful. It made me retch and poor Aldo was sick every time he was made to drink some.

When Mother tried to find out what was going to happen next she was told that we would just have to be patient. The conditions in this refugee institution were completely intolerable. After a couple of days Mother decided we had had enough and announced that she wanted to go back to the Barga area. She was informed that we could not be discharged because we had no visible means of support. We would just have to stay there until arrangements had been made to get us back to England.

It became quite clear that we would not be repatriated in the foreseeable future. It would appear that the only way we would be able to leave that institution would be if we could find an Italian person with private means who would guarantee to finance and look after us. Mother managed to get a message to her aunt Nella. After what seemed like an interminable period of time Nella came along and signed all the necessary papers for our discharge.

Whilst in the refugee camp they had noticed that my shoes were full of holes and practically falling apart. They then issued me with a pair of brand new American army issue boots. They also gave me an official permit written in English to say that I had been issued with these boots by the relevant authorities and that I was entitled to wear them.

What luck! My wish for a pair of brand new boots had been fulfilled. I would have preferred a pair of studded mountain boots but I was nevertheless very grateful. I treasured these boots and wore them almost continuously.

On the day we left the institution I was stopped by the American Military Police. They began to point at my boots wanting to know how I had got them. There was a lot of black market going on at that time in military equipment and they obviously thought that I had illegally acquired the boots. I took out my permit and showed it to the MPs. They perused the document. At first they looked at each other rather bemused and after some discussion, said: "OK", and waved me on.

We now went to stay in Nella's house in the San Donato district of Lucca. Aunt Dora was also living there along with her friend Quinta and her daughter Anna.

Chapter 20

Lucca can trace its origins back several millennia. Archaeological finds indicate that there were settlements there during the Stone Age and the Iron Age. Then it was inhabited by the Ligurians and the Etruscans.

Over the ages it has had a very chequered history. In 180 BC Lucca became a Roman colony. After the collapse of the Roman Empire in AD 476 it was conquered first by the Goths and then in AD 552 by the Byzantines.

During the Middle Ages, Lucca, like many city states in Italy at that time, was involved in frequent conflicts with its neighbouring towns: in this case Florence and Pisa.

After the fall of Napoleon, the Duchy was governed by the Austrians until the Congress of Vienna when it was assigned to Maria Luisa Bourbon. In 1847 the Duchy was ceded to the Grand Duchy of Tuscany and a few years later it was incorporated into the newly reunified state of Italy.

The most striking architectural feature of the city is *Le Mura* (the walls). The first walls were built in the Second Century BC around what would have been a very small area of the present town.

The medieval walls were built in the Thirteenth Century, with four gateways and a moat with a drawbridge. The present day defensive walls are a very imposing structure. They were built between 1544 and 1650. Completely encircling the city, they are over four kilometres long with eleven protruding bastions. They were originally surrounded by a moat and an embankment.

These walls have survived intact. There are now seven gateways into the town. The moat has been filled in, resulting in a wide grassy area all around the city. On top there is a wide avenue which runs the whole length of the walls. In recent years this carriageway has been closed off to vehicular traffic.

The American troops were encamped on the grassy area all around the walls. They were not allowed inside the old city because all the gateways had large notices in red, which declared in English: **Off limits to all Allied Personnel**.

Quinta's daughter Anna and I would set off each day to walk to the outskirts of the city, a journey of approximately 25 to 30 minutes. When we arrived at the city walls we would engage in conversation with the American soldiers. In this way we would try to beg whatever we could in the way of food and other goodies.

I particularly remember the bread. Compared with Italian bread it was very white with a soft crumb and it had a consistency reminiscent of cotton wool. When you dunked this bread in coffee it absorbed an enormous amount of liquid.

The fact that I had a girl with me tended to make the soldiers more openhearted than they would probably have been had I been on my own. They were always very generous to us and the two of us would usually be staggering back with quite a lot of food for the family.

Anna was quite a pretty girl. She had a rather light complexion untypical of the Latin look of an Italian. I thought that she was very cuddly. I rather fancied her and thought that this was perhaps an ideal opportunity to get to know her more intimately.

I had erroneously assumed that she would most likely be a bit of a flirt like her mother. To my disappointment she rejected all my advances and soon made it clear that she was not interested at all. Our relationship became strictly a business affair. I would have to wait till much later in my teens before I managed to have a girlfriend.

Whilst living in Lucca, Aunt Dora had struck up a relationship with an English soldier, a sergeant in the transport section. He would come to the house nearly every day. I learnt later that Aunt Dora had really fallen for this sergeant. In fact she had written to her niece Gina in England informing her that she was very seriously considering leaving her husband Joe and setting up house with her new friend.

Of course, Mother never told me any of this at the time. It was not the kind of news that a mother shared with a young son. In the end, this relationship came to nothing for when her newfound boyfriend moved on with the advancing frontline, Dora decided, in the cold light of day that she could not go through with it after all.

If she had left her husband it would have had serious consequences for her. It was not only the type of action which was completely contrary to her beliefs as a practising catholic, but it would also have soured her relationship with her family and the whole extended Italian community.

We had been in Nella's house in Lucca about three weeks when Mother, who had always had itchy feet, declared that it was time that we returned to the Barga region. However this was easier said than done. Firstly, all the regular forms of transport to that region had been suspended and secondly how were we going to manage to get there because it was forbidden for civilians to travel to the front line. Furthermore, it was quite a long way: about 30 kilometres.

Aunt Dora's boyfriend promised that he would take us and so, one day, he arrived at the house with an army utility vehicle. We climbed aboard and hid in the back of the vehicle whereupon he proceeded to fasten down the tarpaulin very securely.

At Ponte a Moriano there was an American army checkpoint and the English sergeant had warned us to be completely silent when we arrived there. The driver was taking quite a risk, for his actions were contrary to army regulations. Aunt Dora's friend Quinta, who had a reputation for being a bit of a brazen hussy, decided that she would also come along just for the ride. Of course, she insisted on riding in the front.

When we eventually arrived at the checkpoint at Ponte a Moriano the vehicle had to stop at the barrier. We could hear a lot of discussion going on between the driver and the military personnel in charge of the checkpoint. After what seemed like ages we were off again. A little while later the driver stopped at a quiet spot in the road and came to the back to see if we were all right. We were cock-a-hoop for we had indeed made it.

Dora's boyfriend explained to us that the American MPs at the checkpoint had insisted that Quinta was not allowed to proceed any further. She had to get off and the driver was told that he would be able to pick her up on the return journey.

We thought it was quite amusing. Quinta had always believed that she could use her feminine charms to get whatever she wanted. But this time it did not work and Mother and I had a good laugh. On reflection it was probably a good thing that Quinta had come along with us. If she had not done so, the MPs manning the control point might have decided to search the back of the vehicle.

And so we went back to *Le Paradise*. Quite a lot had happened whilst we had been away. Amabile had got rather friendly with a black private American soldier called Carlo. Carlo was well built and over six-foot tall. He had a very large head and was quite ugly. I reckoned at the time that if you suddenly met him in the dark you could die of fright.

Despite his appearance, he came over as being a very gentle and friendly person. He always spoke in a very calm and hushed tone of voice. I got the impression that he wouldn't have harmed a soul. Carlo had really fallen for Amabile and I am sure that he was secretly hoping that it might lead to marriage.

Just before we returned to *Le Paradise*, the Buffalo soldiers had been replaced by a division of white American soldiers. Among these new troops Amabile had found herself a white sergeant that she was really keen on. She reckoned that this might possibly be an opportunity for her to start a new and exciting life in the United States.

Carlo, who was unaware of this new relationship, religiously came to see Amabile each Sunday. Amabile kept up the pretence but it was obvious that there was a difference in her attitude towards him. All the while it was Mother who, on the express instructions from La Tognera, had to keep making excuses in English to Carlo.

Carlo was by now beginning to sense that all was not well. About two or three weeks later he arrived as usual. He asked about Amabile and La Tognera told Mother to inform him that Amabile had gone to church. In actual fact she had gone off for the day with her darling sergeant.

Carlo had brought some washing with him. He then proceeded to take it out of his haversack and got busy doing his laundry by hand. It was a nice warm sunny morning and Carlo was happily singing away whilst doing his laundry at the stone washtub outside.

I had gone to mass at Catagnana that morning and when I returned Carlo began to question me. In broken Italian he asked me if Amabile had gone to church that morning. In my innocence I replied that she had not and that she had really gone away for the day with a white sergeant. When Carlo heard this, his attitude changed completely.

He quickly bundled up his wet laundry and off he stomped in a very bad temper. No one had ever seen him in this mood, but we did not pay any particular attention to it. And so we never thought any more about the incident. In fact La Tognera and Amabile were hoping that this would perhaps mean that they had got rid of Carlo once and for all.

One afternoon, about three days later we had a very strange call from a black GI sergeant. He knocked at the door and asked to talk to Dina Moscardini. Mother then introduced herself. This sergeant started questioning her about her relationship with American soldiers. He started off by asking her if she had been fraternising with Buffalo soldiers. My mother was quite adamant that she had not had any form of relationship with any military personnel black or white.

It was obvious that this sergeant was different from all the other soldiers we had previously encountered. Apart from anything else he had a very distinctive and unusual shoulder flash on his uniform. He clearly disbelieved Mother because he kept on asking the same questions over and over again. By this time Mother was getting rather annoyed at his constant questioning. She was just about to show this soldier the door when suddenly, in the midst of all the interrogation, Carlo arrived and entered the house.

When the sergeant saw Carlo, he took him outside and there ensued a very heated argument between the two men. Eventually Carlo left and the sergeant came in and gave Mother some news which made her gasp with a mixture of fear and astonishment. His first words were: "Madam, you are very lucky to be alive at this moment. It was very fortunate that I happened to be here to save you from certain death. That man Carlo had brought with him a loaded revolver and he had come here with the express purpose of shooting you."

The sergeant was a member of Special Branch and he had called especially to see Mother because Carlo had been boasting to his comrades: "I'm sure going to kill that bitch. Just you watch!" Carlo's comrades all knew what he was capable of and they had thought it best to inform their superiors.

Then the Special Branch sergeant proceeded to tell Mother that, contrary to what he seemed, Carlo was a very dangerous man. He would have killed Mother without as much as batting an eyelid. He had in fact been sentenced to ninety-nine years imprisonment in the United States for killing two security guards and three policemen in armed robberies. He had only been released from prison because he had expressed a wish to serve as a soldier in the front line.

The conditions for his release from jail were that, on his return to the States at the end of the war, if he had survived the frontline, he would have to go straight back to prison to complete his life sentence. And in the United States a life sentence meant just that. There would be little clemency for prisoners who had been convicted of such violent homicides.

Apparently, Carlo had been blaming Mother for Amabile's change of affections. He thought that it was Mother who was influencing Amabile, whereas she was merely translating what La Tognera had wanted her to convey to Carlo. We could not believe what we had heard and, not unnaturally, we were extremely frightened.

We certainly couldn't stay at *Le Paradise* any more. If Carlo was really that wicked there was no telling what he might do in the future. This Special Branch sergeant certainly could not give us any guarantee that Carlo might not try to come back again. Mother decided that there was only one thing to do. The next morning, we moved house.

We went to stay in Barga at a house owned by a Mr Marchetti who was really Mother's uncle. He ran an ice cream parlour, confectioners and tobacconist in Ashington, England. He had purchased this house in Barga with a view to eventual retirement.

An elderly couple, whom we knew as *Il signor Ferdinando* and *La signora Francesca*, were looking after the house. They were living there rent-free in exchange for their services as caretakers. They were really a lovely couple. They were so kind and very understanding when they learnt of our dilemma.

Life in Barga turned out to be quite pleasant. There was a lot more to do there than at *Le Paradise*. As it was not directly in the front line, the Germans did not bother to shell Barga too frequently and we were therefore not so restricted in our movements.

I soon began to make friends with other boys. There were so many places we could visit and we would wander around most of the day amusing ourselves. It was a very welcome relief from the stressful life in the front line. We stayed in the Marchetti house until well after the allied troops had broken through the Gothic Line and advanced towards northern Italy.

Signor Ferdinando had spent some time in America in his younger days. He had been a waiter in a restaurant in Baltimore and he would often spend the odd hour in the garden with me during which time he would tell me all about his exploits in America. He particularly kept emphasising that America was indeed a wonderful land of opportunity.

I never did ask him why he had chosen to eventually settle in Italy but I suspect that he had probably come back to get married and had never got round to returning to the States. His wife was such a gentle person. Perhaps she may not have been keen on emigrating to America. *Signor Ferdinando* would undoubtedly have submitted to her wishes without question.

Towards the end of April there was a lot of troop activity in the area. It certainly looked as though something very important was about to happen. Groups of soldiers were going round visiting every house. All the time they were noting down the numbers of rooms in each house and how many civilians were in effect living there.

The Marchetti house was a two-storey building divided into two flats, one above the other. *Signor Ferdinando* and *Signora Francesca* had always occupied the ground floor flat and they had allowed us to move into the upstairs flat. The military authorities were in fact requisitioning accommodation for their troops and they suggested that we temporarily go and live downstairs with *Signor Ferdinando* and *Signora Francesca* so as to leave the upstairs flat empty for the use of their soldiers.

Two days later, the extra troops arrived en masse. There were literally thousands of them, all Buffalo soldiers. They billeted twenty soldiers in the upstairs flat. They had requisitioned in a similar manner, sections of buildings all round Barga for that same purpose. We were soon to learn the reason for the arrival of so many soldiers. The following morning turned out to be the 'big push', the decisive assault to smash through the Gothic Line.

When dawn arrived the troops left for the final assault. On learning this we thanked God for we thought that at long last the war was over for us. But it was not to be so, for we had to endure one last unimaginable day of horrific bombardment.

As soon as the Germans realised what was happening they knew that they had no chance of holding back these thousands of attacking soldiers. They decided that they might as well vent their wrath on Barga and cause as much damage as they could. So they started to fire off all their artillery ammunition before they retreated. Up till then we had been very lucky in Barga for, at times, several days would pass by without even one shell being aimed at the town.

At about eleven am we began to encounter the most intensive barrage of shelling that we had ever experienced. The shells were fired non-stop until about four pm that afternoon. The continuous noise of these shells exploding near our house and in other parts of the town was deafening and we were absolutely terrified because we were certain that our world was coming to an end.

We spent all that time huddled together under one of the large double beds, holding hands and continually praying that we might be spared. When the shelling eventually stopped our sense of relief was too pleasurable for words. The ensuing peacefulness and lack of noise seemed so unreal at first. Nevertheless it had finally happened. The frontline had gone and we were now safe from the dangers of war.

The Germans had extensively mined the whole of the mountain ridge on the approaches to Lama. This turned out to be quite a problem for the advancing allied troops. The dangers were enormous. With a complete lack of concern for the inevitable resulting casualties the military authorities just ordered the Buffalo soldiers to advance forward regardless. In this way they used the black GIs to clear the minefields. They sent them forward just like sheep. This resulted in a mindless slaughter of human beings, which could very well have been avoided.

Once the front line had moved on, the allies left only a small token force in Barga. For some time afterwards they kept bringing in auxiliary units in order to comb the mountains for bodies. For several months they were collecting the corpses of fallen soldiers and taking them away in body bags. They had to proceed with great care for they had to avoid the numerous live mines still lying around on the mountain slopes.

In Barga, I used to go around with a group of three or four other boys. We were always on the lookout for new adventures and we took advantage of every opportunity to try and beg what we could from the few troops that were still in the area.

One afternoon we approached four Buffalo soldiers with our usual request for chocolate and cigarettes. After giving us some chocolate one of the soldiers conveyed to us in rather broken Italian that they were looking for women. His exact words were: "*Cercare donna; fichi, fichi*". The Italian word *fichi* means figs. In our youthful naivety we at first started to wonder what he wanted with figs. The GI then proceeded to illustrate what he actually meant by using unmistakable body language.

We tried to ignore this but he was very insistent. Then one of us had the 'bright' idea of taking them along to the see the local prostitute Giovanna. Along with the others I thought this was very amusing and I was quietly giggling to myself at the thought. We knew that this *puttana* lived in *Via di Mezzo*, but we were not exactly sure of the precise location.

Off we went into old Barga. *Via di Mezzo* is in fact a very long street. We asked several people and despite receiving some rather strange looks we finally found the house. Unfortunately when we got to Giovanna's house there was nobody in. We kept hammering on the front door to no avail. The soldiers were very disappointed to say the least. They were obviously intent on some form of hedonistic gratification and it was at this juncture that one of them put his arm around me and started stroking my bottom.

At first, I thought that he was just being friendly and showing a normal kind of adult affection towards a young boy. Then I suddenly realised what he was intimating and I went icy cold at the thought. After a bit of a struggle I managed to free myself from his grasp. I quickly shouted to the others: "I don't know what you lot are doing but I'm off home. I suggest that for your own sake you all do the same" and off I went running home as fast as I could.

I took all manner of short cuts through narrow alleyways in case the soldier decided to come after me. Arriving home completely out of breath, Mother asked me what was wrong. I tried to shrug it off by saying that I had just been racing one of the other boys home. I was nevertheless glad that I had reached home safe and sound.

When we all met up the following day I learnt that they had also had a similar experience but had all managed to escape without being violated. We all laughed and joked about it afterwards but I still remember that event with great trepidation.

During that period in Barga I experienced another very disconcerting incident which once again made me go all cold with fear. One day when I was playing in the *Fosso* area of Barga with my pals, I saw this jeep come flying into town. In the jeep were four Buffalo soldiers. I took one look and could not believe my eyes. I looked again but there was no mistake. One of the soldiers was Carlo.

Without hesitation I took to my heels and went running home like the wind. As soon as I arrived there I blurted out to Mother: "*Mamma, mamma, non uscire perché è arrivato Carlo*" (Mummy, mummy don't go out, Carlo's arrived in town). Mother at first was wondering what I was mumbling about. When I repeated my warning in a quieter manner, Mother realised the potential danger. She consequently kept a low profile for a while and avoided going out for a couple of days. Fortunately we never saw Carlo again. He had probably just been out on a jaunt with some of his comrades.

It wasn't long before the local picture hall, the *Cinema Roma*, started opening up again and showing American films. Our little gang of boys had discovered a way for us to get into the cinema free.

One of us would buy a ticket while the others waited outside the emergency exit at the back of the cinema. Shortly after the film had started the person who had bought the ticket would surreptitiously sneak along to the emergency exit, open it from the inside, and all of us would stealthily make our way inside, one at a time, at reasonable intervals. This worked for a little while but the management soon discovered our ruse and immediately put an end to our free movies.

Chapter 21

We remained in Barga for a few more weeks and, towards the end of May, we went back to Sommocolonia. Wanda's house had been quite badly damaged because it was next to *San Frediano* church which had been razed to the ground by a direct hit during the American bombing. In fact most of the houses in the village had been either completely destroyed or extensively damaged. Of the remainder there were very few which had not suffered some form of damage.

Nevertheless, life had to go on and people started moving back into the village. We then moved into a vacant house at *Monte* which comprised of two rooms on the first floor and two on the second floor. The ground floor was just a large basement area with an earth floor. The door to this basement led straight onto the street. Access to the living accommodation was via a rather steep external stone staircase.

As soon as the front line passed, the military authorities at first just abandoned the village leaving behind all kinds of ordnance and ammunition. Most of the ordnance was either damaged beyond repair or had been rendered unusable. A few carbines were found in good working order and these were immediately appropriated by some of the returning villagers. In the *piazza* there was a burnt out jeep. The Americans had obviously managed to negotiate the narrow *mulattiera* with this jeep.

There was ammunition everywhere and a lot of it was very much live. There were lots of caches in the village consisting of rifle grenades, hand grenades and literally boxes and boxes of rifle and machine gun bullets. Most of them were found abandoned in the houses where the allied troops had been stationed during the front line.

The ammunition store in the entrance lobby to the church had obviously gone up when the church received the direct hit. There was another ammunition store in the basement of the house just below *Nonna* Maria's house.

This depot was really scary. Not only was it full of ammunition but also the door leading onto the street had been partially smashed in during the fighting. There were rifles and all manner of ammunition, grenades and hand grenades strewn everywhere and it presented a real hazard to the villagers.

Most of this ammunition was in a precarious state and on the broken door of the basement a notice had been affixed which read: '**DANGER! UNEXPLODED BOMBS.**' Some barbed wire had been stretched across the gaps over the broken door to prevent any stray dogs wandering in. Not unnaturally people were very worried because young children could not appreciate the danger. However it was not till the late spring of the following year that they were finally cleared up by bomb disposal units.

With all those guns lying about everywhere it was not surprising that some of them ended up in the wrong hands. There was a rumour that armed gangs of men had started wandering about the countryside raiding farmhouses. So far, they had limited their raids to isolated farms. Everyone was a little concerned that these gangs might start targeting villages. Sommocolonia would have been particularly vulnerable because at this juncture only about a quarter of the population had in fact returned to live in the village.

Our new abode was situated quite close to Benito's house. As he was now my nearest neighbour we started going about everywhere together. We were always on the lookout for new adventures and some of our exploits were little short of madness.

Benito and I had decided that we would set up our own warning system against any armed gangs. Benito lived two doors away just around the corner and we had agreed on a basic code of words, which we would shout to each other. At the given signal each of us would set in motion whatever plan of action we had devised to defend ourselves. What we were proposing was not only irresponsible but it was also very dangerous.

And how was I intending to fight back in case of a raid? I had decided to arm myself in the following stupid manner. I had hidden two cases of live hand grenades in the spare bedroom on the second floor. If anyone were to knock at the door in the late evening or during the night I would shout and ask for identity. If I could not get any satisfactory answer I would quickly make my way up to the bedroom and surreptitiously peer out of the window.

If what I saw looked like several people standing on the steps carrying what might be rifles, I would just let fly with the hand grenades one after the other. When I think back on it, the plan was sheer lunacy for I hate to imagine what would have happened had it come to a confrontation. Fortunately it never came to that because these armed gangs stayed clear of villages after all. I never let Mother know about these crazy notions because she would have gone berserk at the thought

We now found ourselves in the position of being very short of money again. We no longer had the perks from Mother's interpreting duties. Also there were no soldiers around to give us the occasional handout. Consequently we had to make savings on every possible occasion. It had even got to the stage that, whenever a light bulb blew, I would try to get a few more hours of use by juggling together the two broken ends of the filament. Strangely enough it did work.

I found that the cartridges that had been left lying around everywhere proved to be a good source of making a little money. Benito and I would knock the bullet tops off and collect the gunpowder. This could be sold along with the empty shells which had a fairly good scrap value. Then we would melt the lead out of the actual tops and sell the lead and the copper that remained.

There were three types of cartridge on the machine gun belts: ordinary tops, black tops and red tops. We knew that the black tops were filled with some kind of explosive so we threw these away. The red tops of course were tracers.

At first, we threw away these red tops along with the black tops. Then I figured that there must be some lead in them to give them weight, otherwise they would not travel very far. So one evening I filled an empty metal machine gun ammunition box with red tops and put this on a roaring fire in the living room to melt down the lead in the usual way.

It took a long time for the tops to get hot and it was not until the metal machine gun box started glowing red with the heat, that things started to happen. Suddenly there was a loud pop and one of the bullets came flying across the room. This was followed by another and another until they all started popping off in all directions.

We had to quickly evacuate the house and wait until all the bullets had gone off. We then had to also wait for part of the night to make sure that it was safe to go back into the house. All told it was quite a hair-raising experience. We were lucky that the house did not burn down. Fortunately we had very little furniture in the room. Also the fact that the floors were tiled turned out to be a blessing.

Mother was not very pleased. By now I was rather too big to be smacked. But she chastised me very severely and I was in her bad books for several days. After that I stayed well clear of red tops.

The two houses either side of ours were both uninhabitable because of the extensive damage they had sustained. On one side was the house where the veteran GI had been manning the heavy calibre machine gun. There wasn't any live ammunition but there were lots of spent cartridges. These heavy calibre shells were quite weighty and they were a good source of money. Benito and I spent several days digging around the ruins looking for them.

The house on the other side was very badly damaged. The whole of the front had vanished and all one could see were the other three walls that were still standing, with the damaged floors to the upper storey hanging down precariously. This house had also been occupied by GIs and, despite the obvious danger, we would, from time to time, go rummaging among the ruins in the hope of finding something useful. We never found any shells here but we occasionally came across a few American cigarettes.

There were also many hand grenades lying about that had just been abandoned by the troops. Benito and I would often go up into the *Rocca* and throw the odd grenade into the well to amuse ourselves. On reflection it was really lucky that none of us boys came to any harm from these activities. I did in fact once have a narrow escape when I injured my hand and this taught me to leave all ammunition alone in the future.

Mother was still pestering the military authorities about going back home to England. One day, towards the end of June, we received a message from an allied colonel in Barga that a refugee train would be passing through Pisa within the next two days and we were authorised to join it. So we quickly packed our bags and Mother was convinced that we were going home.

When we joined the train at Pisa we got quite a shock. Most of the rolling stock in Italy had been either destroyed or damaged by the retreating Germans as part of their razed earth policy. They had also blown up most of the main line tracks. Although the carriages of this train were passenger coaches, they were completely gutted and consisted of nothing but empty shells. Inside, it was just one large empty compartment, and the people were sitting and lying around everywhere on the floor.

The journey itself was a nightmare. There were no facilities for washing or toilets, and conditions were absolutely disgusting. The civil authorities had so far only been able to lay a single track. As this refugee train was of the lowest priority we had to continually spend many hours on sidings at railway stations all along the route in order to allow more important traffic to pass.

The stations themselves were still in a state of disrepair and the sanitary arrangements were minimal. The demand on the limited toilet facilities whenever we stopped at stations was enormous and one can imagine the sordid state of these latrines after a while.

Our destination was Naples and the journey from Pisa to Naples took five days and five nights. It was a nightmare journey that I would never like to undertake again. On arrival at Naples we were bundled into military trucks and taken to a small town called Aversa, a few miles north of the city. Our final destination was a refugee camp at the edge of the town.

The refugee camp at Aversa had been a lunatic asylum before the war. It was situated on the periphery of the town and it consisted of large institutionalised buildings offering hardly any privacy at all. However this did not really bother us for we thought we would soon be going back to England.

The running of the camp was in the hands of the allies. The financing was under the auspices of the United Nations. Inside the camp there were refugees of many different nationalities. I should think that every nation in Europe must have been represented there, and one could hear people speaking in many different foreign languages.

After a day or two we learnt that some of the refugees had already been in this camp for some months. We now began to think that perhaps we might not be setting sail for England in the very near future.

It was the start of summer and it was beginning to get quite hot. The inhabitants of Aversa were not the cleanest of people. They thought nothing of just dumping their rubbish in the street and there were piles of garbage lying everywhere. Because of the heat, the smell was quite unbearable at times. In fact the allies patrolled the streets on a regular basis. They went round spraying all the mounds of rubbish with DDT powder in order to prevent any outbreaks of disease. They wore masks as they went about their duties.

Mother let me wander around the town on my own. During the short period that we were there I managed to get along twice to the Saturday morning matinée at one of the cinemas. These matinées were geared for children and youths. I distinctly remember the two films that I saw on those separate occasions.

The first film was 'The Sullivan Family'. This was the story of an Irish-American catholic family and their five children, all boys. These boys were inseparable throughout their childhood and adolescence. When America entered the Second World War the Sullivan boys all volunteered for the navy. They wanted to serve on the same ship. At first they were refused because the regulations expressly forbad siblings to serve on the same ship in wartime.

The Sullivan boys kept insisting and eventually the naval authorities relented. During a naval battle in the Pacific their ship was hit by enemy fire. Sadly, all five of them lost their lives. It was a most enjoyable film and a real tearjerker. I don't think there was a dry eye in the cinema at the end of that film.

The other film was 'Sergeant York' starring Gary Cooper. At the beginning, the film was a little slow for a children's matinée. Towards the end of the film when Gary Cooper finally enlisted into the Army and managed to capture all the German troops with his crack shot skills, the whole teenage audience burst into shouts and yells of appreciation. Although we did not literally raise the roof, I am sure that the noise must have been heard several streets away.

Mother was getting fed up with staying in this refugee camp. It was obvious that there was no chance of us going back to England in the near future. She then started pestering the authorities again. When she got no joy from the Camp Commandant she went into Naples to badger the higher military authorities and British consular officials.

I remember sitting next to a Buffalo soldier in the cab of an enormous military truck bombing down the road between Aversa and Naples. This happened on several occasions. Sitting high in the cab of a large military lorry travelling at some considerable speed on a straight road was great fun. The warm breeze would be whistling through our hair and the experience was quite exhilarating.

All these trips into Naples were of no avail. Not only was there no sign of a ship to take us back to England but the powers that be could not guarantee how long we would have to wait in the refugee camp.

By the end of July, Mother decided that we had been in this refugee camp far too long already, so she made plans to get us back to our little village in northern Tuscany. By persistently pestering the commandant of the refugee camp, she managed to be issued with an official pass from the military commander of the region. This pass authorised us to travel on any train on our journey back north.

And so we gathered together our few personal belongings and made our way to the railway station at Aversa. It was late afternoon and the first train that arrived was a goods train, which was guarded by British soldiers. Towards the centre of the train there was one passenger carriage. This carriage was completely undamaged.

The station platform was packed with potential travellers and everyone rushed forward towards the solitary passenger carriage. They were soon to be disappointed because the armed guards prevented everyone from boarding the train. Then Mother made her way forward and challenged the guards in English.

Their reply was that this was a special goods train, which was out of bounds to all civilians. Mother was not to be put off by this and she thrust forward our special permit. I think they were rather taken aback by Mother's persistence. There followed a long period of discussion and argument between Mother and the British guards.

Eventually, they gave way to Mother's unyielding persistence and we were allowed to board the train. Apart from the six British soldiers, we were the only people on the train and we were able to choose a compartment all to ourselves. Here, we settled down into what was indeed great luxury.

We had been travelling for about an hour or so and night was starting to fall, when suddenly all hell was let loose as someone started firing a gun. One of the guards came in to inform Mother that armed bandits were attacking the train. Then, he advised us to lie down on the floor for our safety. There seemed to be bullets flying everywhere outside the train and after what seemed to be ages the train entered a tunnel and the firing stopped.

When the train emerged from the tunnel one of the guards came back and told Mother that the armed bandits had managed to unhook the last two freight wagons and had got away with UNRRA goods worth well over 5 million lire. It was at this juncture that we learnt that this train was laden with relief UNRRA foodstuffs and clothing. UNRRA stood for United Nations Relief and Rehabilitation Administration.

One of the major functions of this United Nations organisation was to "plan and arrange for the administration of measures for the relief of victims of war in any area under the control of the United Nations through the provision of food, fuel, clothing, shelter and other essential necessities." The United Nations had set up this body in order to supply aid relief to those nations in Europe, which had been ravaged by the war. And Italy certainly qualified to receive aid in this manner.

The following afternoon, when the train pulled into a goods station in Rome it was immediately surrounded by American Military Police. They announced that we were under arrest for colluding with the bandits who had robbed the train. The British guards were nowhere to be seen. They had obviously disappeared and all the shooting on the train had been nothing but a screen to hide what had undoubtedly been a well-planned scheme for the soldiers to rob the train along with their civilian accomplices.

No wonder they didn't want any witnesses on the train. They most probably would have got away with their story had it not been for us travelling on the train. The most likely explanation for their disappearance was that they had gone AWOL to avoid being arrested for their role in helping the 'armed bandits'.

Meanwhile, Mother was subjected to a lengthy period of questioning by the Military Police. At first they did not believe her. After a lot of hassle she was eventually able to persuade the Military Police that we were merely innocent bystanders who had just happened to be travelling on that train. If Mother had not been able to speak fluent English and thus argue her case in unequivocal terms, we would most probably have been arrested and spent some time in a military jail.

Now we had to get back to Tuscany. There were not many trains like the last one, which had passenger carriages, and we travelled back to Lucca on several different goods trains.

Two days later we reached Lucca station sitting on the outside platform of a brake van. We arrived early in the morning cold and hungry and exceedingly dirty. We made our way to Nella's house in the San Donato district of the town. There we received a warm welcome from Dora and Nella. Dora's friend Quinta had gone back to Barga several weeks earlier. Dora on the other hand had remained behind to keep Nella company.

The first thing we did was to get washed and afterwards we had breakfast. Then we had a well-needed sleep. We remained in Lucca for a couple of days. During that time we went to visit a lady called Irma who was my mother's cousin. She lived in the centre of the old town quite close to Puccini's birthplace. Her flat was on the top floor of a four-storey building. It was quite an old building and the steps up to the flat were very steep.

Irma was a widow with five children, two boys and three girls. She had had quite a struggle to bring up such a fairly big family on her own. Several years later we established much closer ties with this family when my brother John and Irma's eldest daughter, Raffaella were married.

Whilst we were here I was able to wander around the city centre each day. It was really fascinating to observe the hustle and bustle of everyday life in a city like Lucca. Commercial trade was getting back on its feet and a stroll down *Fillungo*, the main shopping thoroughfare, was very interesting. This street was lined with very fashionable shops displaying goods, which had expensive price tags. Everybody seemed to be merely window shopping and I never did see anyone make an actual purchase.

*Ruins of 'San Frediano' church, Sommocolonia. Completely destroyed
by American aerial bombardment on 27 December 1944.*

Lt.John Fox, US Army. Hero of the battle of Sommocolonia.

John Fox's stone marker.

*Bernard Moscardini with John Fox's widow, Arlene Fox, and his
sister Jane Fox Pope. Photo taken in the year 2000 in Sommocolonia.*

The temporary foot bridge in Barga. Built by Brazilian forces to
replace the road bridge blown up by the German Army.

Bernard Moscardini sitting on the ruins of 'San Frediano' church.
Photo taken by Jock Tricki in October 1945.

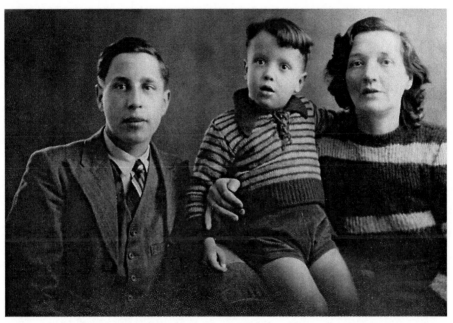

Bernard Moscardini with Mother and Aldo. Photo taken shortly after their return to the UK in 1946.

Chapter 22

After a couple of days' rest we made our way back to the Barga region. Dora, who had been residing in Lucca for some months now, decided to return to Sommocolonia with us. The Nardini brothers had started running their thrice-weekly service between Barga and Lucca again. And so we boarded the *corriera* taking with us the few belongings that we still possessed.

When we arrived in Sommocolonia Dora took one look at the conditions in the house at *Monte* and declared that she would not be staying there. That first night she had to sleep on a makeshift mattress in the second bedroom. This bedroom had no furniture at all. Mother and I were not particularly fond of the house either, but we had no choice because there was nowhere else that we could go.

The next day Dora moved down to Barga and went to stay with a friend called Romola. Romola was originally from the village. She had married a man from Barga, and had been living there for several years.

Meanwhile Father, who had been interned in the Isle of Man, had been released. Although he had never been a paid up member of the Fascist party he had always been a very ardent admirer of Mussolini. He would never compromise in his beliefs and because of his stubborn stance in this matter he was in fact one of the very last internees to be released.

Whilst he was interned in the Isle of Man, Father had been allowed to write to us now and again and so we had received the occasional letter informing us that he was well. It was on the strength of these letters, that Mother had been able to prove to the Italian authorities that Father was an internee. This had enabled her to be granted the small *sussidio* (pension) from the Italian Government.

Father went straight back to Bedlington Station and after some negotiation with the authorities he managed to regain possession of his shop premises. Of course this meant that the temporary British Restaurant run by the Local Council had to close. Little by little Father was able to acquire the various licences necessary for trading. Conditions in Britain in the immediate post war period were very difficult. Most products were very strictly rationed and all businesses were severely restricted.

He found trade extremely difficult at first. Tobacco and confectionery products were on strict quota. This quota was supposed to be dependent on one's pre war volume of trade. As all Father's business records had been destroyed there was no way that he could substantiate any claim based on his pre-war turnover.

Consequently he was granted a very small quota at first. His ice cream business was starting to really take off. Ice cream was a luxury, which had been almost unobtainable during the war. Father soon found that he could have sold ice cream non-stop all day and every day. Unfortunately sugar was very strictly rationed and because of this Father could make ice cream for only a short period each day.

Father was now sending us the occasional parcel of clothing. It was very exciting to receive these parcels for we never knew what we might find inside. I particularly remember that in one of the parcels there was a trench coat. To say that I was delighted to receive this coat was an understatement.

The coat seemed to have flaps and pockets everywhere. Although it was a little long for me, Mother soon had it shortened by the local tailor. I then began to wear this 'prize possession' everywhere. I was very fond of this trench coat and I used to flaunt it with great pride whenever I went down to Barga.

Back in Sommocolonia, life did not seem to have changed much in the few weeks that we had been away. However, a few more people had in fact returned to live in the village and there was a fair amount of activity going on. Everywhere people were starting to repair their damaged houses in order to make them habitable again. Sadly very few of the houses that had been completely destroyed were rebuilt.

The house around the corner, which belonged to the lady called Catera, was being repaired. I would go and watch the builders at work. One day I asked the builders if there was anything I could do to help. They said that I could transport wheelbarrow loads of sand from the pile where it had been delivered by the mules to the worksite about fifty yards away. I would be paid the handsome sum of five lire a barrow load.

This seemed like a great way of making money, but I was soon to realise that this was not as easy as it sounded. The wheelbarrow was a very large one and I had to fill it up to the top. Consequently, after about only two or three barrow loads I was absolutely exhausted. I then decided that the work was far too heavy for me.

Meanwhile, us boys were still messing about with ammunition. One of our daring exploits would be to hammer off the end from a rifle grenade. As soon as we removed the top we would quickly grab the detonator inside and throw it away when it would explode with a harmless bang. What an insane thing to do for if we had ever misjudged what we were doing we would have surely been killed.

After removing the detonator we would be left with the stump end that was normally slotted onto the rifle. The inner part of this section was a short barrel with a firing pin at the bottom. I reckoned that if I were to insert a machine gun cartridge into this barrel and bang the whole section against a hard stone the firing pin would fire off the cartridge.

It really worked and I found it very useful with tracer cartridges, for you could follow their trajectory right up into the sky. This was particularly spectacular at night.

When I had perfected this extremely dangerous operation I thought I would boast of it to the builders. So I climbed the external stone staircase outside Catera's house and said to the builders: "Watch this." I put a cartridge into the barrel and let fly and felt very proud when they expressed their approval at following the path of the tracer bullet into the sky.

Then I felt something very warm on my hand and, looking down, I noticed that there was blood everywhere. Unfortunately, the barrel was slightly shorter than the cartridges because the top inch or so protruded without any protection. Consequently, on firing, the top section of the shell splayed outwards. It was a piece of the shell, which had shorn off and gone straight through the top of my hand that had caused the wound.

I got very frightened and didn't know what to do. Luckily, my uncle Fiore had been working near by and he soon appeared on the scene. He took me to the public fountain where he washed my hand under the tap. Then he wrapped a towel tightly around it and declared that he would have to take me to the doctor's surgery down in Barga.

Of course there was only one way to get to Barga: we had to walk. All the while I was very worried about what was going to happen to my hand. And then how was Mother going to react to this. All of a sudden the future looked bleak.

We arrived at the surgery in the late afternoon outside surgery hours. The doctor, who was called Serafini, was none too pleased to have to be called to open up the surgery especially for me. When he heard that I had wounded myself fooling around with ammunition he was even less sympathetic to my predicament. Instead of trying to put me at my ease he proceeded to give me a sermon.

He then started to unwind the bloody towel and I got a terrible shock when I saw that my hand was swollen to twice its normal size. Apparently, the two holes where the piece of shrapnel had pierced right through the flesh had closed over and the wound was full of blood.

After taking off this temporary bandage Dr Serafini tried to open the wound so that he could medicate it. He gave it a squeeze and nothing happened. Then, after squeezing it very firmly the wound suddenly burst open and the blood spurted out straight onto the doctor. His face was now all covered in my blood.

At this he wiped off the blood with a towel. Then he began a tirade of cursing and swearing which would have made a trooper blush. All the while he was chastising me about my stupid behaviour. He was completely oblivious to the fact that I was in constant pain. He now started a programme of exploring inside the wound with a surgical instrument. He was looking for shreds of metal as he informed me. I was not given any kind of anaesthetic and whenever I protested about the excruciating pain he just told me to be quiet because I had brought this upon myself.

When the doctor was satisfied that there was nothing inside the wound, he began to disinfect it and, after stitching up the holes, he bandaged my hand thoroughly. I was then informed that I would have to keep my hand raised at all times in a sling. He said I would have to return to the surgery the following day to check up on the progress.

Dr Serafini was a very blunt man who was never afraid to speak his mind. His philosophy in life was a rather basic communist philosophy. He invariably refused payment for his services when treating his poorer patients. His richer clients were charged extra to compensate for this.

Whenever he went shopping he would just go and help himself to goods and inform the shopkeepers to put it all on his bill. The local tradesmen dreaded him coming into their premises for they knew that he never had any intention of settling his bill.

I remember years later when I met him whilst on holiday in Barga, he asked me if I had any English cigarettes. When I took out my packet of cigarettes he just grabbed it, emptied half of them into his hands and, without even thanking me, waved an acknowledgement with one hand and walked off.

He never struck me as being the healthiest of men. He was grossly overweight and he was an inveterate chain smoker. He would only remove the cigarette from his mouth if he had to perform some delicate medical 'operation'. He was always coughing and yet he incredibly managed to live until well into his early seventies.

Fiore decided that I was not up to undertaking the five kilometre climb on foot to Sommocolonia, only to have to return down to Barga the following day. I certainly felt very shaky after that ordeal in the doctor's surgery.

He then suggested that it might be better if I stayed in the Marchetti house with *Signora Francesca* and *Signor Ferdinando*. In actual fact this house was very handy for it was situated just around the corner. It was only a two-minute walk away but when I arrived there the bandage was full of blood and obviously something was wrong. I then had to go straight back to the surgery.

When doctor Serafini saw the bloody bandage he just casually said: "Right, let's have a look." After unwinding the bandages he realised that although he had stitched up the two holes, he had left a little bit of gauze sticking out at one end. This was acting as a wick for the blood to ooze through. He then had to unstitch the wound, and scrape around inside again to make sure there was nothing left there. Then he stitched it up fully again and bandaged me up a second time.

Despite the fact that I was in terrible pain and was obviously very frightened, the doctor had no sympathy for me whatsoever. He just kept repeating that it would teach me a lesson. And that it certainly did for I never touched another cartridge or any other item of ammunition after that.

Signora Francesca and *Signor Ferdinando* were very good to me. They never chastised me for what I had done, but rather expressed great regret at my mishap. Staying with them was probably the best thing that could have happened to me. They treated me like a son and were extremely kind almost to the point of spoiling me. This was just what I needed to give me the strength of mind to overcome this latest misfortune of mine. I stayed with them just over a week before going back to Sommocolonia.

Had I gone straight home to Sommocolonia Mother would most likely have chastised me and continually nagged me about the accident. She came to visit me the next morning and seemed pleased to see that I was all right.

In the afternoon I went back to the surgery accompanied by *Signora Francesca*. The doctor unwound my bandages, took one look at the wound and declared that all was fine. Then he said: "Right young man, come back and see me in a week." This time his language was very restrained for he couldn't very well curse and swear in front of this sweet little old lady.

On my visit to the surgery the following week the doctor seemed pleased with the progress of the wound. I was now declared to be well on the mend. There was no need for me to go back to see the doctor. Of course if there were any problems I would have to return to the surgery immediately.

By now I was also feeling a lot better. The constant pain had gone and the wound was now mainly sore rather than painful. And so after about ten days I was well enough to go back home to the village.

When I got there I was surprised to see that Mother genuinely welcomed me back. I suppose some time had passed since the accident and she had got over her original anger at my foolishness.

I was really lucky that everything turned out well. There had been the fear that I might have lost the use of several fingers. At first they were unusable but the movement returned little by little. The only after effect of my injury was that every so often the wound could be slightly painful depending on the weather. With the passing of time this got less and less and nowadays there is only the scar to remind me of the accident.

Chapter 23

I had certainly learnt a salutary lesson. I got rid of all the ammunition in the house and I never fooled around with any kind of explosives again.

Life in the village had settled down into its normal daily humdrum routine. We were getting near the end of the summer, and we now began to resign ourselves to spending another winter up in the mountains, for we seemed no nearer to getting back to England.

That autumn all the schools reopened. The schoolmistress, Signora Cassettari, came back to live in the village. Orlando was due to start at the *Scuola Superiore* (Upper Secondary School) in Barga at the beginning of October. Signora Cassettari persuaded Mother that I was quite a capable pupil and that I should attend the *Scuola Superiore* along with Orlando.

The *Scuola Superiore* was certainly a lot more demanding than the *Scuola Media*. For a start we had a fair amount of homework on a regular basis. Then we started learning other languages besides Italian.

Latin of course was compulsory. By tradition the only foreign language taught in secondary schools in Italy had always been French. However the *Scuola Superiore* in Barga was for the first time providing a course in English as an alternative to French. The number of places on this course was very limited and the demand was very high.

I quite naturally opted for English instead of French. I reckoned that I had an indisputable case for learning English. The logic behind my reasoning was as follows: I would be going back home to England sometime in the fairly near future and I would need some knowledge of English. Fortunately I was successful and I was allocated a place in the English group.

Orlando was his usual moaning self. He was always complaining about the amount of homework we were given. He really was quite an indolent little toad as far as academic work was concerned. I on the other hand found the *Scuola Superiore* quite enjoyable. I had always liked being stretched academically and I found this new challenge really stimulating.

At the end of September one of the villagers was involved in a fatal accident. Mr Biondi the bee expert had gone out looking for mushrooms. He had been warned by everyone in the village not to go anywhere near Lama. He reckoned that if he kept to the slope near the edge of the ridge just below Lama he would be all right. Unfortunately he stepped on a mine and was killed instantly.

His family of course were devastated. Paolo had been wounded in the *piazza* the previous October and it seemed that the family was fated. They had to undergo yet another disastrous misfortune. The following March, the eldest son Adelmo was killed in the *piazza* by an unexploded shell.

Adelmo had noticed two young children who were playing with a shell. He had been in the Forces during the war and he immediately recognised the danger. He went over to the two children and persuaded them to hand over the shell. As he was carefully carrying it away to a spot where it might be safely detonated it suddenly went off. The explosion blew a big hole in his stomach and he died before help could arrive.

In October, we had a surprise visit. We received word that one of Mother's cousins, Jock Tricki, had arrived in Barga. In peacetime, Jock ran an ice cream parlour in Ryhope, County Durham. He was now serving as a staff car driver in the British army in Italy. He had arranged for four days leave so as to come and see us in Sommocolonia. We were greatly excited when we heard the news and off we went, Mother and I, to meet him in Barga.

Jock was a short chubby fellow and not the fittest of men. I soon realised that he was struggling to carry his kitbag up the mountain track. I then took the kitbag off him, slung it over my shoulders and set off at a fair pace up the *mulattiera*. Even then I had to keep slowing down in order to allow Jock to keep up with me.

Jock was undoubtedly an optimist with a very positive outlook on life. He was a very jolly chap and he was always laughing. Every now and then he would just say to mother: "Eeh Dinah pet. It's lovely to see you." One of my first questions to him was: "Have you brought any English cigarettes?" His reply was: "Yes, 400."

My whoops of joy soon turned to disappointment when I learnt that he had brought Craven 'A' cigarettes. Not Players or Capstan, but Craven 'A'. They were a very distinctive brand of cigarettes because they had a cork tip. I was not very keen on this cork tip for I reckoned it imparted a strange taste to the cigarette. Cork tips are not to be confused with filter tips, for filter tips were seldom used on cigarettes at that time. Jock had also brought some Cadbury's milk chocolate, which was especially welcome.

I took him around the village to show him all the damage that had been caused by the war. He was absolutely astounded at the extent of the devastation. When we started recounting to him our experiences during the frontline he could not believe that so few civilians had been killed or wounded. He reckoned that we had all been extremely lucky to come out of it alive.

We really enjoyed Jock's company. Sadly, his stay in Sommocolonia soon passed and we settled back into our normal monotonous daily routine. There was no news on the repatriation front and we had to resign ourselves to spending another winter in the mountains.

In Barga the two bridges that had been blown up by the retreating Germans were being rebuilt. The job had been entrusted to a local builder. The small footbridge had already been finished and the main road bridge was due to be completed early in November.

The day was fast approaching when the *Comune* would be officially declaring the bridge open. All that needed to be done was to remove the wooden scaffolding, which had been supporting the new structure during its rebuilding.

When the day arrived and the scaffolding was removed, the bridge collapsed. There ensued a terrible furore. Accusations were made that the builder had been cutting corners and using inferior materials.

The upshot of it all was that the builder was immediately arrested for defrauding the local *Comune*. Another builder had to be found to rebuild the bridge once again. This time the work was given to a larger and more reliable firm. In the end the local builder's low estimate for the work had turned out to be more expensive. This certainly illustrated the truth of the saying that 'you only get what you pay for!'

My main present for the feast of the Epiphany was a new pair of trousers. At that time there was a very limited choice in ready-made clothes. Most of the time people would buy a length of cloth and have their clothes made up by a local tailor.

This was to be my first pair of long trousers. I chose to have a pair of plus fours because they were all the vogue among adolescent boys in that area at the time. By then I was well past my fourteenth birthday and I thought that I was very grown up in this wonderful new pair of plus four trousers.

Somehow Mother had received word that a troopship would be calling into Naples in the near future. In all probability we might be able to get a passage back home on that ship. If we wanted to be considered we could not afford to put off any decision to travel.

Mother didn't hesitate for we had been waiting a long time for an opportunity like this. In early January, we set off again, this time by coach. The journey was a very pleasant one and completely different from the one the previous summer.

On the coach the seating was very comfortable and, whenever we stopped for refreshments, the food seemed to be marvellous. For lunch that first day we stopped at a roadside *osteria*. I remember that we had fried pork sausages. They were so succulent and tasty that I still have a clear memory of their excellence. Even the weather seemed to be smiling on our good fortune at last, for the sun was shining and it was quite mild for the time of year.

Our destination was the refugee camp in Aversa again. When we arrived we were extensively interviewed. After ascertaining that we were eligible for repatriation they informed us that we would be having a series of inoculations. We then knew that this time it was for real: we were at last going back home. Our delight at the prospect of finally being repatriated made the unpleasantness of the inoculations seem insignificant.

About ten days after our arrival Aunt Dora and several other Anglo-Italians from the northeast of England joined us. We were all very thrilled to see Dora. Now she also had to go through all the catalogue of interviews, medical examinations and inoculations

One day early in February, we were told to pack up all our belongings for we were off. We were transported by lorry to the docks in Naples where a ship, was waiting for us. The ship was the Dunnottar Castle, a liner belonging to the Union Castle Line, a steamship company which, during peacetime, specialised in running regular services between the UK and South Africa.

Along with many other liners, the Dunnottar Castle had been requisitioned by the British Government for use as a troopship during the war. On this run, it was in fact taking home British troops from the Far Eastern theatre of war. The steamship had come from Port Said and was calling into Naples to pick up Italo/British civilians who had been blocked in Italy during the war in Europe. What a wonderful sight this ship was. It was indeed a luxury liner!

As soon as we arrived on board our family was split up for the following reason. Women and children were allocated cabin accommodation, whereas men were to be billeted in the lowest deck of the ship. As I was not far from my fifteenth birthday I was classified as an adult and had to join the men in the hold.

The seas were still mined and we were all issued with lifejackets in case of emergency. On the first day out to sea, they held an exercise to rehearse the 'abandon ship' procedure in case we hit a mine. It had all been explained over the loudspeaker system with the emphasis on the fact that it was just a routine drill.

Because my knowledge of English was very poor at the time, I did not understand the information given out over the loudspeakers. I consequently took the blaring of the sirens to be a real emergency. I immediately started to panic because instead of going to the allocated muster station I went looking for Mother and Aldo. After what seemed like endless wandering around the ship, I finally found them and Mother reassured me that it was only a rehearsal.

In the hold, the accommodation was one large extensive open area with tables spaced all around. We were allocated fifteen to a table. Everyone was issued with a hammock. These were to be our beds. We were shown how to sling these hammocks and most of us tried them. Then, after falling out of them a few times, everyone decided that it would be easier just to lie down on the hammocks in a corner of the deck.

The food was brought in large containers and each table was allocated a certain quantity of food, which we had to share out among ourselves. On the first day there was barely enough to go around and most of us could have eaten more. We need not have worried, for as soon as the ship set sail fewer and fewer people turned up for meals because of seasickness. As the journey progressed, there were even fewer people each day and when we were finally approaching the end of the voyage, there were only four people still eating at our table.

One of the passengers in our group turned out to be a very bad sailor. In fact he spent the whole of the eight day voyage to the UK being constantly seasick and by the time we docked in England the crew were getting really worried about his state of health.

I personally found the food absolutely wonderful. English food was a great relief from the monotonous fare we had been living on for the past five years. I particularly liked the puddings. In fact I ate so much that I am sure that I put on weight during the voyage.

The only downside in my opinion was the fact that a very large amount of food had to be thrown overboard because so many people were seasick throughout the voyage. All the tables were affected and I was one of the very few people who were not ill during the journey. After having to suffer great hunger during the war, it seemed like a cardinal sin to throw away so much good food.

On board there was a holiday atmosphere everywhere. The troops were returning to old 'Blighty' to be demobbed and the civilians were being repatriated back home. Everyone was in a happy mood and no one even thought of the dangers of the mined seas. Fortunately, we were lucky not to encounter any mines.

Every afternoon, there were tombola sessions and the shop on board even sold chocolate bars. This together with the fact that I was able to scrounge innumerable cigarettes from the troops made it a memorable journey for me and the eight day voyage from Naples to Southampton was like a luxury cruise. The Bay of Biscay was particularly rough on this crossing and many people were affected by it. I didn't mind the rough weather; on the contrary I thought it was great and enjoyed the heaving of the ship.

After a very enjoyable 'cruise' the liner arrived in Southampton. Mother, who had been perfectly well during the voyage, suddenly started feeling seasick just as we were docking.

At Southampton, we had to go through all the immigration procedure: filling in forms and extensive questioning. After going through all these formalities, we were allowed to officially enter the UK. My father and my uncle Joe were there to meet us and there followed a very emotional reunion.

The first thing that Father did was to give both Aldo and me a Mars Bar each, which we immediately started to eat. I was not very impressed with this chocolate bar for I found it very rich and rather sickly. It certainly didn't taste as nice as the delicious plain milk chocolate we had on the ship. I didn't want to disappoint Father so I told him that it was lovely.

We then went on to London by train. I was particularly struck by the fact that one of the electric trains in the Southampton area seemed to have no visible means of propulsion. It was only later that I learnt that, unlike Europe, the few electric trains in the UK at that time got their power from a central electrified rail just as at present on the London Underground.

In London, we stayed in a boarding house near the centre. I was very fascinated by the gas geyser in the bathroom and kept turning on the hot water tap to watch the flames suddenly come shooting on. That evening we went out to eat at Gennaro's Italian restaurant and we had a wonderful Italian meal.

The next day we went by taxi to King's Cross station to catch the train to Newcastle-on-Tyne. At Newcastle, my uncle Dino, mother's brother, was there to meet us. Half of us got into his car and the other half into my uncle Joe's car and we were taken to Newburn-on-Tyne where we had another emotional reunion. Waiting to welcome us were my aunt Eva and my cousins Gina, Iolanda and Dino. The latter was always referred to as 'little Dino' in order to distinguish him from his father.

My aunt Eva had prepared a slap up Italian meal, including *maccheroni*, to celebrate our arrival. There followed a lengthy convivial *cena all' italiana*. In fact I thought we were never going to come away from the table.

That night we went to stay in Blaydon at my aunt Dora's house and, the following day, my uncle Joe drove us to Bedlington Station.

My initial feelings at being back in Bedlington Station were rather mixed. I was very happy that we had finally returned. And yet I had this strange feeling of unreality, as though it were all a dream. That evening when I went to bed I was a little apprehensive that perhaps the following morning I might wake up to find myself still in Sommocolonia.

The next morning we had a surprise visitor. At about 9.30am there was a ring on the doorbell. When Mother went down to open the door, my faithful friend, Kenneth Thompson, was standing on the doorstep. He had come to welcome me back. I then knew that we were indeed back home. "*La vacanza era finita*" (the holiday was over).

Epilogue

When Paolo Biondi closed his restaurant, the fortunes of the lovely village of Sommocolonia began to experience an ever-spiralling downturn. Mr Vincenti, who owned the bar and shop, together with all the special licences, passed away shortly afterwards and the business was taken over by his eldest son Peppe. Peppe unfortunately was an alcoholic and after about five or six years he decided to close the business completely.

This now meant that the village would be without either a shop or bar. Several of the villagers, including the parish priest, Don Piero, and Father, who had retired to N*onno* Bonafede's paternal home at *Monte*, decided to band together to form a cooperative. They each bought shares in a village cooperative and, after being granted the requisite licences, set up a bar and small *bottega* (shop) in the village *piazza*.

At first this new venture really prospered for a while. However, as some of the older villagers began to die, interest in the cooperative started to wane and there was talk of winding it up altogether.

Then, as the population of the village continued to decline, the new purpose built school became very badly under subscribed. The local *comune* decided that it would be far more economical to bus the handful of children of primary school age to the larger school in Barga. The authorities then proceeded to close the primary school in Sommocolonia, along with many other village primary schools in their region.

Then the *comune* very foolishly proceeded to sell off all these empty school buildings, a course of action, which I gather, was regretted later on. Had they rented out these school premises instead of selling them, they would have retained some control over their future.

An outsider called Bruno bought the village school from the *comune* for a song. He immediately started to use these premises to house a band of foreign workers whom he employed as loggers and general labourers.

When it looked as though the village cooperative was about to close Bruno stepped in and bought the shares at a knock down price, thus taking over the *bottega* and bar in the *piazza*. Everyone looked upon Bruno as a saviour but he turned out to be just an opportunist.

After about two or three years he transferred the bar to the school premises, which he had previously purchased. He traded here for a year or two and when he got fed up with running a business which took up a lot of his time, he just closed both the bar in the school premises and the general food store in the *piazza*.

As a consequence Sommocolonia is now a dying village without a shop or a bar. So there is really no venue where the inhabitants might socialise or congregate. There are now barely 60 inhabitants and the majority of these are of pensionable age.

Most of the empty houses have been sold as holiday homes to foreigners from England and America. Others have been bought by Italian city dwellers. Thus the village only really comes alive during the three summer months of June, July and August. At other times of the year it is almost like a ghost town. Unfortunately it looks as though this decline is destined to continue until the village might become completely uninhabited

Il Terremoto del 1902

Nel millenovecentdue precise

il dì cinque di Marzo, la mattina,

un terremoto a noi ci diede avviso

fece tremar la camera e cucina.

E questo crollamento all'improvviso

che fa tremar la grande e piccolina

uomini, donne, tutti in un momento

saltano il letto lesti come il vento.

A dir la confusione e lo spavento

che ciascuno provò quella giornata,

pareva che cadesse il firmamento

perciò resta la casa abbandonata.

Si forma all'aria aperta un reggimento

d'una popolazione addolorata

Sommocolonia, addio, dove andrai

che questa volta disfatta sarai.

Di terremoti ne veniva assai

che lungo il giorno ne venne ventotto.

Quello che spaventò noi più che mai

o Redentore mio, fu quello delle otto.

Di camini caduti rimirai

ma grazie a Dio nessun ci restò sotto.

Quello che spaventò a ciascun la fronte

vedendo torba l'acqua della fonte,

E le persone nella piazza pronte

che sembrava il Giudizio Universale,

pareva che cadesse tutto il monte

ognun di noi ci si guardava male.

Trema la terra come fosse un ponte

perciò si va alla chiesa parrocchiale

fiduciosi si andiede tutti avanti

a cantar litanie di tutti i santi.

Però in chiesa non si sta restanti,

processionando ce ne andammo in Rocca,

la processione fu di tanti e tanti

che di cuore il gregar sortia di bocca.

Così si prega tutti tremolanti

quando la morte la camicia tocca,

e dopo che il pregar fu terminato

devoti si ritorna sul sagrato.

Il popolo devoto è spaventato

intorno al prete si mette in colonna

fiduciosi in Maria sapete è nato,

la voce si sente d'uomo e di donna.

Molto pericoloso è il nostro stato,

devoti ricorriamo alla Madonna.

Se scosse forti più non sentiremo

stasera tutti in chiesa torneremo,

Fermo proponimento ora faremo

di entrare in chiesa in piena devozione.

Gesù con la Madonna pregheremo,

speriamo Iddio ci rechi salvazione.

Se poi ci salva la Madre beata,

Domenica in paese sia portata.

La sera la funzione fu suonata.

Senza temenza ognun si reca in chiesa

a pregar Maria nostra avvocata,

che nei perigli è la nostra difesa.

Il sole aveva fatto la passata,

l'aria notturna sopra a noi distesa.

La gente per le vie si disperava,

stare in casa nessun si fidava,

la piazza più che mai si appopolava;

di passare la notte è l'intenzione

e della legna il popolo portava

onde si accese un grosso focarone.

Qualcuno nella notte se ne andava,

prendendo alloggio in qualche capparone.

A dire il vero, tutti appassionati,

la notte si passò da disperati,

spesso da terremoti tentennati:

ma grazie a Dio venivano pianino.

A giorno chiaro siamo ritornati

ma spaventati come Musolino

di nuovo alla chiesa radunati,

grazie chiedendo al Redentore Divino.

Queste sono giornate per pregare

e non si parli più di lavorare,

è passata la voglia di mangiare.

E poi del pane non se ne trovava,

i Barghigiani fecero scappare

e pane a Barga non si fabbricava.

In questi giorni il mormorare

che spesso e volentieri si mormorava

un gran peccato è la mormorazione,

dunque si cessi in tutte le persone.

E chi di mormorar da la ragione

ora sarebbe di troncar la via,

e peccatori facciamo attenzione

che è tempo di pregar Gesù e Maria.

Il giorno sesto Marzo è terminato

lievi scosse si senton raramente

ma di cuore ciascuno avea pregato

che Iddio le manda tutte leggermente.

Ecco il settimo giorno a noi presente.

Chi non darà retta a questo mio sermone

si troverà pentito in agonia.

Se il popolo da Dio vien castigato

è sempre per cagione del peccato.

Attraverso la memoria sempre lucida di Marchetti Rosa (Annetta) di
Sommocolonia, ultranovantenne, siamo
riusciti a ricostruire questa bellissima poesia, scritta
dal poeta del paese (Pierucci) nel triste evento del
terremoto del 1902.

Firmato Vincenti Carlo

The 1902 Earthquake

It was in 1902 precisely

on March fifth in the morning

that we were all apprised of an earthquake

which caused bedroom and kitchen to shake.

And at this sudden quake

which frightened all, big and small,

men and women suddenly

sprang like a shot from their beds.

Because of the confusion and fright

which everyone experienced on that day,

as it seemed that the very heavens were falling,

we therefore all abandoned our homes.

In the open there gathered a whole horde

of residents full of sorrow.

Goodbye Sommocolonia, where are you heading

for this time you will surely be destroyed.

There were many tremors indeed

for on that day we experienced thirty-eight.

The one which frightened us most

o my Redeemer, was the one at eight in the morning.

I could see many chimneys fallen

but thanks to God none was buried thereunder.

What frightened us all was the fountain

for it gushed forth muddy water.

And the people all stood ready in the square

as though it were the Last Judgement.

It seemed as though the whole mountain was falling

and we all looked at each other quite sadly.

The earth was shaking like a rope bridge

therefore we all made for the Parish Church.

Full of faith we wended our way

chanting the Litany of the Saints all awhile.

However we did not linger there inside

but processed our way up to the Rocca.

There were so many of us in procession

that we were greatly alarmed.

And so in trepidation we were all praying

as though death were already touching our tunic.

And after we had prayed at length

we faithfully returned to the sacred area of the church.

The devout populace all a feared

around the priest in columns duly assembled.

All were trusting in Mary,

and one could hear the cries of men and women.

We are all in a state of great peril,

and devoutly have recourse to Our Lady.

If we don't experience any more strong shocks

we will all return to the church this evening.

Now we will make a firm commitment

that we will enter the church in full devotion.

We will pray to Jesus and Our Lady

and hope that God will spare us.

If our Blessed Mother were to save us

on Sunday she will be carried in procession.

That evening the bells announced the service.

Fearless we all assemble in the church

to pray to Mary our Advocate

who is our Protector against all dangers.

The sun had sunk over the horizon

and the nocturnal air was now descending.

The people were wandering about in despair

for none trusted staying in their houses.

The piazza was crowded more than ever

the intention was to spend the night there.

And everyone was bringing wood

whereupon a large fire was duly lit.

Some went off into the night

to seek some safety out in the open.

To tell the truth, full of grief,

all spent the night in awesome fear,

frequently shaken by earthly tremors;

but thanks to God they only came slowly.

Now that we have returned to break of day,

but still frightened to death,

we gather once more in the church,

giving thanks to our Divine Redeemer.

These are truly days for prayer

and no one is talking of work,

for we have even lost the desire for food.

Besides there was no bread to be found

for in Barga all had run away

and so no bread was being baked.

In those days there were many grumbles,

so many of us were frequent and willing moaners.

For grumbling is a great sin

which should be desisted by all.

And for those who have succumbed to complaining

now is the time for all to stop.

And let us sinners realise

that it's time to pray to Jesus and Mary.

The sixth of March has now come to its close

and weak shocks are rarely felt.

But we had all wholeheartedly prayed

that God might only send light tremors upon us,

now that we have reached the seventh day.

Those who do not take heed of my warning

will soon be full of agony and sorrow,

for if the people are to be punished by God,

it will, as always, be because of sin.

Through the memory of the very lucid mind of the
nonagenarian Marchetti Rosa (Annetta) of Sommocolonia,
we have been able to reconstruct this very beautiful
poem written by the village poet (Pierucci) on the
occasion of the 1902 earthquake.

Signed Vincenti Carlo

Lightning Source UK Ltd.
Milton Keynes UK
29 November 2010

163615UK00003B/217/P